Hands Off!

70 Active Learning Strategies
for Massage and Bodywork Education

Virginia S. Cowen, PhD

Pennate Press

Copyright © 2020 Virginia S. Cowen

All rights reserved. This product is protected by copyright. No part of it may be reproduced in any form including information and storage retrieval systems, electronic, mechanical, photocopying, or recording without written permission from the publisher.

ISBN 978-1-953891-10-5

Cataloging-in-Publication Data

Cowen, Virginia S., author
Hands Off! 70 active learning strategies for massage and bodywork education / Virginia S. Cowen
ISBN 978-1-953891-10-5

Library of Congress Control Number: 2020919648

Product or corporate names which may be trademarked are included for informational purposes only with no intent to infringe.

First printing November 2020

Published by
Pennate Press
An imprint of IngeniousWellness
P.O. Box 83
Piermont, NY 10968
www.pennatepress.com

Preface

It is no secret that students in massage and bodywork education often see peer practice as a reward for sitting through courses in science and theory. Hands on classes are active learning. They demand engagement from students. Quite a different experience from sitting in a lecture.

Hands on classes are not the only opportunity for active learning in massage and bodywork. Almost any topic can be crafted into a quality learning experience that gets students on their feet, interacting, and doing something. Active learning strategies can help students retain and apply information.

I have been working in and around active learning for a long time. I have seen everything from strict approaches to team-based learning to games used as formative assessments. I do like a good, meaty lecture. But I also enjoy fun activities that do not make the work of learning seem obvious.

This book started out as a list of fun things that could engage students in the shift to distance learning that occurred during the coronavirus pandemic. I heard from many instructors who moved lectures online because they did not know what else to do. I thought a list might help think about experiential learning to help anxious students and stressed instructors interact with each other and have fun while learning. The list quickly grew into a book. As I began to sketch out ideas, I realized that there were ways to adapt many strategies for different topics and learning environments. The result was a reference book with variations and ideas for implementation to help instructors get inspired to try engaging instruction.

I hope that instructors and students can have fun and valuable educational experiences with active learning.

Virginia S. Cowen, PhD

Contents

Preface i
    Contents iii
Introduction 1
    Curriculum and Instruction 3
    Instructional Design 4
    Planning 6
    How To Use This Book 8
Kinesthetic Activities 13
    Strike a Pose 14
    Dance Break 16
    Simon Says 18
    Calisthenics 1 20
    Calisthenics 2 22
    Calisthenics 3 24
    Mime Time 1 26
    Mime Time 2 28
    Mirror, Mirror 1 30
    Mirror, Mirror 2 32
    Puppet Master 34
    Silly Walks 36
    Strong or Flexible 38
Observational Activities 41
    Sports Stars 1 42
    Sports Stars 2 44
    Sports Stars 3 46

Dancers 1	48
Dancers 2	50
Musicians 1	52
Musicians 2	54
Famous Statues	56
Fashion Models 1	58
Fashion Models 2	60
What am I?	62
Dolly and Me	64
One-Minute Paper	66
Collaborative Activities	69
Daisy Chain	70
Minus One, Plus One	72
Rowing Team	74
Dominos	76
Connect the Dots	78
Strips in Sequence	80
Plus or Minus	82
Project-Based Activities	85
Where a Client Might Look	86
Simple Questions	88
Physical Assessment Protocol	90
Psychosocial Assessment Tool	92
Study Skills	95
Create a Study Guide	96
Not Quite Open Book	98
Wiki Me This	100
Short Videos	102

CONTENTS

- Infographic 104
- Fix My Class Notes 106
- Mind Your MCQs 108
- Peer Teaching 111
  - Fuzzy or Clear 112
  - I Could Teach That 114
  - A Little Help Here 116
  - What Did I Say? 1 118
  - What Did I Say? 2 120
  - Explain that to Grandma 122
- Games 125
  - Name that Term 126
  - Zebra or Horse? 128
  - Mnemonics 130
  - Tennis 1 132
  - Tennis 2 134
  - Hangman 136
  - Match Game 138
  - In a Flash 140
  - Got Your Back 142
  - Poker 144
- Team-Based Learning 147
  - Jigsaw 1 148
  - Jigsaw 2 150
  - Debate Club 1 152
  - Debate Club 2 154
  - Debate Club 3 156
  - Team Quiz 158

HANDS OFF!

Case-Based Learning 161
    Clinic Role-Play 162
    Threaded Case Scenario 164
    Case Across the Curriculum 166
    Creative Case Scenarios 168
Appendix 175
    Appendix A: Sample Lesson Plans 176
    Appendix B: Sample Assessments 180
    Appendix C: Ideas for Reflection or Evaluation 183
Index 185
About the Author 189

Introduction

HANDS OFF!

Active learning is the purposeful engagement of students in the educational process. Instructional strategies that are experiential, experimental, or otherwise participatory provide students with the opportunities for engagement with course material. In massage and bodywork education, active learning typically is reserved for hands-on practice. Passive learning is used in didactic courses and students are left on their own trying to integrate content.

In a passive learning model, the instructor is positioned as the expert, and the student as the novice. The expert presents information to the novice often via lecture and assigned reading. Assessments in the form of tests or assignments are used to measure the extent to which the students are familiar with course material. This traditional format can provide evidence that a student recalls information, but it can make it challenging for the student to apply material to solve a problem. The combination of lectures and tests is a passive learning model for students. It places a heavy burden on instructors in several ways. Extensive time is needed to prepare lectures, create tests, and to give individual feedback to each student in class when tests are graded.

There are a wide range of active learning strategies that can promote review, application, and integration of course material. Feedback is built into active learning when students learn from each other. Activities can be used for informal and formative assessments. In massage and bodywork education there are ample opportunities for active learning outside of practice sessions. Developing active learning sessions does not necessarily require more time than preparation of lectures and tests. It can save time over the longer term when assessments are incorporated into the activities.

Active learning that requires students to collaborate, cooperate, seek information, and find solutions promotes critical thinking. Involving students in a process that reviews, reinforces, and applies concepts helps them to naturally integrate material from didactic and hands-on courses. It can also help students identify their own knowledge gaps. Opportunities to self-assess and reflect provide students with informal feedback on a regular basis. Massage and bodywork education offers opportunities to incorporate active learning To Engage Students throughout the curriculum.

INTRODUCTION

Curriculum and Instruction

In education for healthcare professionals and providers, traditionally didactic courses have been separated from clinical activities. Didactic courses are cognitive, relying primarily on lectures, readings, and written tests. Clinical education is different in that it is experiential, involving the psychomotor and affective domains. For activities using role-play, peer interaction, and practice sessions, students are expected to draw upon foundational material learned in didactic courses. However, there is evidence that it is difficult for students to retrieve and utilize foundational material and apply it in a clinical context. A potential contributing factor is the different instructional approaches used to present material. Using active learning strategies throughout the curriculum is one approach to help students make progress to master material.

Knowledge Progression

Benjamin Bloom's Taxonomy of Educational Objectives is a well-known model that outlines the progression of learning in the cognitive domain. Knowledge, comprehension, application, analysis, synthesis, and evaluation are areas of learning that can also be viewed as a hierarchy for the complexity of course content. It is not enough for a student to be able to regurgitate information. Rather, students need to be able to recognize, recall, and utilize information by engaging with course material to explore issues or solve problems.

Activities used when material is introduced can help students become comfortable with terms, definitions, and concepts on a general level. More complex activities can be used to promote critical thinking when material is applied and integrated. Building these ideas into a course, or an overall curriculum helps map the learning progression from the level at which information is introduced to where it is utilized. In order to effectively utilize information, students must be led through the progression of review, application, and integration. This can be accomplished with active learning strategies.

HANDS OFF!

Learning Domains

Use of movement, role-play, discussion, reflection, research, and other participatory approaches are student-centered because they engage students in different domains of learning: cognitive, psychomotor, and affective.

The *cognitive* domain involves thinking. This goes beyond simple repetition of information to recognize different levels of learning and use of didactic information. Bloom's Taxonomy is often used to provide a framework for lesson plans, particularly learning objectives that increase in complexity from introduction through mastery of information: knowledge, comprehension, application, analysis, synthesis, evaluation.

The *psychomotor* domain is kinesthetic. It includes movement, motor skills, and coordination. The psychomotor domain also includes touch (the haptic sense) and the ability to sense by using touch (feeling.) Teaching and learning in the psychomotor domain fundamentally involves observation, imitation, and practice. On a more advanced level, the psychomotor domain also includes adaptation when the student makes adjustments to a skill or movement.

The *affective* domain involves feelings and perceptions. It includes interests, attitudes, and emotions expressed through receiving, responding to, and valuing information. This is the domain where professionalism comes into play.

While hands-on practice emphasizes the psychomotor domain, massage education is more than the ability to execute hands-on techniques. Comprehensive learning includes integration of didactic course content with professional demeanor from the intake through the treatment to follow up including documentation. Recognizing opportunities for student engagement at all stages of this learning process can help to embrace different learning preferences while at the same time reinforcing course material.

Instructional Design

Successful active learning requires instructors and students to be engaged in the activity. It can be challenging to take fun activities seriously, so instructors need to set a tone and work to manage the classroom. Training students to take active learning seriously is essential for any activity to be a

INTRODUCTION

success, so selecting where and when to include active learning strategies requires careful consideration.

Students can work individually, in small groups, or as teams. Activities can involve movement, observation, collaborative activities, project-based activities, study skills, peer teaching, games, team-based learning, and/or case-based learning. As students get used to active learning formats, it can be very rewarding. There are different ways to incorporate active learning strategies in a class.

Flipped Classroom

For face-to-face or online synchronous courses, a flipped classroom can be used to engage students. A flipped classroom requires students to complete preparatory work prior to class, and then during class they apply, practice, or engage in creative activities. In order for this instructional strategy to be effective, students may need incentive to prepare for class.

Experiential learning, similar to a lab, provides an opportunity for an applied or kinesthetic experience. Movement and motion can be used to help students embody information from anatomy & physiology or kinesiology. Collaborative activities, role-play, and team-based learning can foster communication and leadership skills.

The flipped classroom is often already used for online asynchronous courses that require viewing recorded lectures prior to participation in discussion forums, but additional active learning strategies can be implemented to engage students in other ways. Creative projects, peer teaching, games, and even movement activities can make asynchronous classes more interactive.

Formative Assessment

Activities can be selected to provide students with the opportunity for formative assessments. Self-assessment naturally occurs during activities when students recognize how well they know material and are able to apply concepts. Instructors can informally assess by observing student participation. Assignments that are products of active learning can also be used as assessments of student performance.

Because active learning requires students to show evidence that they know, can apply, or synthesize material, activities provide an opportunity for instructors to informally assess the class as a whole. Giving students the chance to ask questions, seek clarification, and use resource material can help them become more proactive and self-directed in their learning.

Review

Active learning strategies can provide an excellent format for review sessions. Often review sessions involve students asking questions that are answered by the instructor. Structuring activities so that they require review of material makes review more student focused. Collaborative activities, games, and peer teaching can cover a large amount of material. Case-based learning that poses complex problems also has potential to cover a large amount of material while requiring students to apply and integrate knowledge. Games, movement, or observational activities can help students recall and remember information through the combination of visual, verbal, auditory, and kinesthetic cues.

Planning

Organization and planning are more important than creativity in active learning. Pairing an activity with course material and a learning outcome does not require creativity, just lesson planning. A feedback loop can be used by asking students to identify individual learning objectives before the activity. Then at the end of the activity they can be invited to reflect on how well they met their own learning objectives. To select a suitable activity, begin with course content and learning objectives for a session. Necessary materials should be secured, class space laid out, and an adequate description of the activity prepared. Once students become familiar with certain types of activities, those can be repeated with different content.

Instructional Time

Active learning does not require more—or less—classroom time than conventional teaching methods. Strategizing and preparation can take time for instructors who are new to active learning or are teaching a new course. Starting small can help instructors become skilled at managing a class. Leave adequate time at the beginning of class for pre-briefing. This should include directions, formation of groups, and defining roles. All details about materials students are expected to produce (i.e. summary, document, or presentation) should be included in the pre-briefing. As students get used to active learning sessions, the amount of time needed for pre-briefing will decrease.

Facilitation

Active learning sessions can seem chaotic, so facilitation is essential to keep students on-track and on-task. Regardless of whether students are working individually or in groups, instructors should observe, answer questions, give in-the-moment feedback, and (where applicable) recommend resources. Instructors should be accessible during the activity.

For face-to-face classes, being present in the room and moving around to observe creates informal opportunities for interaction without interruption of the activity. This is not the same in online classes. For synchronous online sessions being visible on camera, responding to questions posed verbally or using the chat feature does convey presence. But the opportunity for casual interaction and feeling instructor presence is diminished unless the instructor makes effort. Instructor presence in the asynchronous environment needs to be more purposeful since there is a lack of direct communication. Monitoring student attendance (i.e. log ins) and reviewing student participation is not easily sensed by students. Communicating with them during learning activities by contributing feedback, asking for clarifications, and making suggestions conveys a sense of presence. Because active learning aims to be student centered, the instructor should be visible but can be in the background.

Reflection and Debriefing

At the end of the active learning session, the instructor should bring the class together to draw the activity to a close. This should be brief, succinct, and reference the objectives of the activity to stress relevance to the course. The instructor can summarize the activity and review the objectives. Then a few individual students or a spokesperson for a few groups can share a reflection with the class. The instructor can summarize how the material covered fits into the overall course. If a feedback loop was used, students can be asked to write a brief self-assessment on how well they met their own objectives. Additional ideas are presented in the Appendix.

HANDS OFF!

Evaluation

Evaluation of an activity is important to gain insight from students about the activity and how it contributed to learning. It can also help to identify aspects of the activity that could be enhanced or improved. Brief surveys can be completed immediately after the session.

How To Use This Book

The core of this book is divided into chapters that include different types of active learning strategies: kinesthetic, observational, collaborative, project-based, study skills, peer teaching, games, team-based learning, case-based learning. Within the chapters, each activity has a summary that includes a brief description of the activity along with details for execution. Materials needed and instructional approaches will differ for face-to-face and distance-learning formats. The Appendix provides information and examples of lesson plans to help instructors with ideas for active learning implementation.

Some topic areas are better-suited to different types of activities. Most active learning strategies can be adapted to different stages of learning. Recognizing diverse needs of students is essential to create inclusive and culturally competent activities. A general summary is provided here, specifics are listed for each active learning strategy.

Materials and Implementation

A range of materials can be employed to facilitate active learning. For each activity, materials needed, implementation ideas, and modifications are listed. Some activities are not suited for all learning environments. A double dash ("--") is used to indicate an activity that cannot be modified or delivered in a particular format.

For **face-to-face** classes, whiteboard, sticky notes, and flip charts with markers can be used for whole-class activities or small groups. Blank paper, notecards, pens/pencils can be used for individual or group activities. Laptops, tablets, or smartphones (with internet access) can be used to search databases for reference material. Smartphones or tablets can be used to make videos.

For **online synchronous** or **online asynchronous** courses, the materials will be contingent upon what is available in the learning management system.

This can include presentations, discussion forums, breakout rooms, whiteboards, wikis, quizzes, games, and different ways to share student-prepared documents, presentations, and/or videos.

Topic Areas

Massage and bodywork education involves courses that use different titles depending upon the institution. Specific course content varies depending upon requirements of each licensing or certification board. In recognition of this variety, the topic areas for active learning were collapsed into five general topic categories:

— Anatomy & physiology
— Kinesiology
— Pathophysiology
— Clinical reasoning
— Ethics

While it is easy to think of using a movement-based activity for kinesiology and a cognitive activity for pathophysiology, switching this around can substantially enhance learning. For example, *Silly Walks* is a movement activity that can be used to review motor disorders in pathophysiology. *Fuzzy or Clear* is a peer teaching strategy that could be used to review kinesiology concepts.

The laboratory component of traditional anatomy & physiology courses includes a range of instructional approaches that involve active learning exercises: observation of models, dissection, tissue testing, etc. If anatomy & physiology is taught without a laboratory, active learning strategies can be used instead to provide students with experiential and experimental learning. *Simon Says*, *Dancers 1* and *Dolly and Me* are examples of activities that can be used to help students review and apply anatomy & physiology concepts through experiential learning.

Role-play is an active learning strategy that is often used in ethics courses to have students observe, model, or work through solutions to issues. When ethical dilemmas cannot be adequately covered in role-play, other active learning strategies can be useful. *Dominos*, *Create a Study Guide*, and *I Could Teach That* are creative ways to help students review and make meaningful connections with topics in ethics.

HANDS OFF!

The variety of topics that comprise massage and bodywork education provide an array of opportunities to get students involved and engaged with course material—beyond simply practicing hands-on techniques. Active learning strategies can help students remember, analyze, and synthesize information from different areas in the curriculum. As students learn to work in a self-directed manner, it can plant the seeds for lifelong learning.

Learning Stage Adaptation Examples

This book provides suggestions to adapt each active learning strategy to three different stages in the progression of learning: review, application, and integration. All activities are not suited to each stage. Examples of activities are provided to spark ideas and help instructors get started. However, this book is not intended to be prescriptive for each and every scenario. When an instructor identifies a gap or need at a specific learning stage, selection and implementation of an activity can help students bridge a knowledge gap.

Using active learning to help students ***review*** material can provide ways to recognize and utilize information that is more meaningful than simply trying to memorize and recall. *In a Flash* and *Got Your Back* are two games that use fun and creative approaches to go through terms and Definitions. *Clinic Role-Play* requires students to identify and extract essential information. *Explain that to Grandma* helps students define terms by requiring them to rephrase a complicated concept and avoid jargon.

Application of course material and concepts requires students to be able to make connections and solve problems. Activities can be structured to help students make sense of abstract ideas. For example, when students have difficulty with muscle anatomy, an activity like *Puppet Master* and *Fashion Models 2* can be used to connect origins and insertions with actions and movements. *Rowing Team* can be used to help students explore ways that different terms relate to each other. *Creative Case Studies* provides an opportunity to extract information from a source and use it to develop a cohesive scenario.

Integration occurs when students utilize material and concepts from different areas in a curriculum. Using active learning strategies can be helpful, especially when the activity involves a game. *Connect the Dots* can be used to organize anatomy & physiology terms. *Daisy Chain* can be structured to

INTRODUCTION

have students work through a complex disease or disorder. The game aspect of the activity can make the content seem less daunting.

It can be especially useful to use an activity to review material and then revisit it later in the curriculum with the goal of application or integration of material. *Calisthenics 1* is a movement-based activity that can be used for a review of joint movements. It can also be used with the goal of having students integrate joint movements with concepts from kinesiology. *Sports Stars 1* is another movement-based activity that can be used to promote understanding of kinesiology concepts. It can also be used to encourage strategies to support clinical reasoning.

Diversity Considerations

When choosing active learning strategies, the needs and abilities of the students must be taken into account. That means inclusiveness for physical disabilities, learning disabilities, and English-language learners. It also requires balancing needs of slower learners with overeager or overachieving students. Care in composing small groups can help to create balanced opportunities for all participants when slower learners are paired with higher-achieving students. This is especially important for peer learning and collaborative activities.

Students in massage and bodywork, like other areas of higher education, have different levels of academic preparedness. Using active learning for formative assessments provides opportunities for the instructor to assess student performance. If remediation is necessary, that can be identified in a low-stakes way that is less risky than waiting for a higher-stakes assessment like an exam. When needed, students who need help can be identified early and directed to supplementary materials, tutoring, or other resources.

Depending upon the characteristics of the surrounding community, students may come from different cultures and socioeconomic backgrounds. Collectively, this means that students may have different expectations, knowledge, and attitudes. They can also have different communication styles, collaboration approaches, and willingness to speak up in class. Activities that allow students to leverage or highlight their own culture or background can contribute to cultural competence for the class as a whole. That may arm the students with knowledge and skills to better serve their community in the future.

Kinesthetic Activities

Strike a Pose

Have students take turns assuming a pose in front of the class to act as a model. The rest of class analyzes the position of the body using concepts from anatomy and kinesiology. For novice learners, this can be done with the instructor guiding the class to look at specific areas of the body (e.g. the shoulder or hip joint.) After students are comfortable with this activity, they can follow a sequence (e.g. from feet to head) to analyze the position.

This activity is good for quick reviews, to demonstrate rapid recall, and to encourage familiarity in using movement and anatomical terminology.

Materials and Implementation

Students should wear clothing and footwear that permits movement.

Face-to-Face

This activity works well in face-to-face classes.

Online Synchronous

Students can demonstrate poses for each other using a webcam.

Online Asynchronous

Students could take turns serving as a model by uploading a photo of themselves in a pose to a discussion forum for other students to analyze.

Topic Areas

Anatomy & physiology

Kinesiology

Pathophysiology

Clinical reasoning

KINESTHETIC ACTIVITIES

Learning Stage Adaptation Examples

Review

Identify where an area of the poser's body is in relation to the coronal, transverse, or sagittal plane.

Basic positions of joints (e.g. what is the position of the right elbow?)

Agonist muscles used to produce a joint position.

Antagonist muscles that are elongated to accommodate a joint position.

Review kinesiology concepts: base of support, center of gravity, types of levers.

Application

Complex joint positions with analysis agonist and antagonist muscles involved in relevant actions.

Identify a movement that could come before or after the pose to create a logical movement sequence.

Integration

List active or passive insufficiencies that might make it difficult for someone else to assume the same position.

Identify diseases or disorders that might make it difficult for someone else to assume the same position.

Diversity Considerations

Some students may not be comfortable being the center of attention, so they may be reluctant to serve as the poser.

HANDS OFF!

Dance Break

Separate the class into two groups. One group dances while the other group observes. Play some fun dance music while the dancers keep dancing until the instructor stops the music. When the music stops, the dancers must freeze in position. The other group analyzes the position of their bodies using concepts from anatomy or kinesiology.

This can be a fun activity to help the students review, and a stress reliever when they get to dance and listen to music.

Materials and Implementation

Students should wear clothing and footwear that permits movement.

Face-to-Face

This activity works well in face-to-face classes.

Online Synchronous

This can be easily executed with students using webcams with a small group of students. To keep the discussion organized, the instructor might need to call on observers so that all students can participate.

Online Asynchronous

--

Topic Areas

Anatomy & physiology

Kinesiology

Pathophysiology

Clinical reasoning

Learning Stage Adaptation Examples

Review

Identify where an area of the poser's body is in relation to the coronal, transverse, or sagittal plane.

Basic positions of joints (e.g. what is the position of the right elbow?)

Agonist muscles used to produce a joint position.

Antagonist muscles that are elongated to accommodate a joint position.

Review kinesiology concepts: base of support, center of gravity, types of levers.

Compare and contrast open-chain and closed-chain joint positions

Application

Complex joint positions with analysis agonist and antagonist muscles involved in relevant actions.

Identify a movement that could come before, or after the pose to create a logical movement sequence.

Integration

List active or passive insufficiencies that might make it difficult for someone else to assume the same position.

Identify diseases or disorders that might make it difficult for someone else to assume the same position.

Diversity Considerations

Some religious and spiritual groups prohibit dancing.

Using music from different genres and cultures can be interesting.

HANDS OFF!

Simon Says

The playground game *Simon Says* can be useful to help students review muscles, joint movements, and kinesiology concepts. The instructor tells students to demonstrate a specific movement. Sometimes the instruction is prefaced with "Simon says…" and other times not. The students should only execute a movement when the phrase "Simon says" is used. If a student moves when the instructor does not say "Simon says," then that is considered incorrect.

This can be played like a knockout game. Any students who make the wrong movement or move when the instructor does not say "Simon says" are considered out of the game, and sit down. The other students keep the game going until one student is left.

Materials and Implementation

Students should wear clothing and footwear that permits movement.

Face-to-Face

This activity works well in face-to-face classes with all students participating.

Online Synchronous

This can be easily executed with students using webcams.

Online Asynchronous

--

Topic Areas

Anatomy & physiology

Kinesiology

KINESTHETIC ACTIVITIES

Learning Stage Adaptation Examples

Review

Contract a specific muscle to produce a movement (e.g. Simon says: flex your right biceps brachii.)

Perform a funny movement (e.g. Simon says: flex your knees but not your hips)

Application

Demonstrate closed or open chain joint positions (e.g. Simon says: show me an open chain position of the left leg.)

Perform a movement that engages a muscle or muscle group in a certain way (e.g. Simon says: show me eccentric contraction of the quadriceps muscle group.)

Integration

Perform a complex movement (e.g. Simon says: Show me any combination of two movements in the sagittal plane that also involve a wide base of support)

Diversity Considerations

Struggling students may feel bad if they lose. They may become disinterested when they have to sit out. Using positive reinforcement can encourage these students.

HANDS OFF!

Calisthenics 1

Calisthenics are repetitive movements using a person's own body weight to exercise. They are also movements that can be used to create a movement-based review. In this activity, students take turns demonstrating calisthenics while the remainder of the class analyzes movements.

Ask a student volunteer to start demonstrating a specific exercise at a comfortable pace. The instructor calls out one joint and the class needs to say the movements for that joint repeatedly in real time during the demonstration. The class can chant the movement to change the pace to have the demonstration speed up or slow down.

Materials and Implementation

The students who volunteer to demonstrate should wear clothing and footwear that permits movement.

An exercise mat is needed.

Face-to-Face

This activity works well in face-to-face classes.

Online Synchronous

This can be easily executed with students using webcams. To keep the activity organized, a single student could analyze while another performs calisthenics.

There should be adequate space to move comfortably and view students from the camera's position.

Online Asynchronous

--

Topic Areas
Anatomy & physiology
Kinesiology

KINESTHETIC ACTIVITIES

Learning Stage Adaptation Examples

Review

Ask a student volunteer to perform jumping jacks, then direct the class to describe movement at the shoulder (abduction, adduction), hip (abduction, adduction), and knee (flexion, extension.)

Application

After the class describes the movements, have them review and antagonist muscles involved in the movements (e.g. biceps brachii and triceps brachii in a push-up.)

Do this activity in a series. Ask the student volunteer to select a calisthenics exercise that is connected in some way to what the previous student did. After the movements have been described the class has to successfully guess the connection (e.g. knees are flexed during a squat and an abdominal curl-up)

Integration

Ask the students to discuss or demonstrate a variation that would vary base of support (for standing exercises) or change the load on a joint/lever (for exercises that are seated or lying down)

Link a repetitive stress injury or injury pattern associated with this exercise to a potentially helpful massage technique or stretch.

Diversity Considerations

Students who are not physically fit may be reluctant to serve as the demonstrator or may have difficulty sustaining the exercise. Modifications to exercises can help accommodate that so everyone participates (e.g. perform push-ups against a wall or with knees down.)

Calisthenics 2

In this version of the calisthenics activity, all students exercise. This activity begins with the instructor calling out a familiar exercise. The whole class engages in the movement. While they are moving, the instructor calls out a joint. The students need to describe the action or position of that joint while they continue to perform the exercise.

Materials and Implementation

Students should wear clothing and footwear that permits movement.

Face-to-Face

This activity works well in face-to-face classes.

An exercise mat is needed.

Online Synchronous

This can be easily executed with students using webcams. Exercise mats are needed. There should be adequate space to move comfortably and view students from camera position.

Online Asynchronous

Students could be assigned an exercise that they film themselves demonstrating and describing. The videos can be uploaded to a folder for the class to compare and contrast in a written forum.

Topic Areas

Anatomy & physiology

Kinesiology

KINESTHETIC ACTIVITIES

Learning Stage Adaptation Examples

Review

The class performs lunges while describing the movement of one joint before switching to another (e.g. focusing on the knee, the students say flexion every time they lunge and flex the knee.) For a face-to-face class they can walk in a circle moving clockwise around the classroom. For an online class, they can stand facing a webcam.

The class can perform regular partial curl-ups (e.g. extension of the vertebral column occurs in the lowering phase of the movement.)

Application

Introduce a variation to an exercise and have the students analyze how it changes. Examples:

— Regular abdominal curl-up vs. oblique abdominal curl-up
— Regular push-up, one-handed push-up, or plank

Integration

Have the students describe kinesiology concepts in addition to muscle and joint movements. Example: the difference in center of gravity that occurs when performing toe touches.

Link a repetitive stress injury or injury pattern associated with this exercise with a massage technique or stretch.

Diversity Considerations

Students who are not physically fit may be reluctant to participate or may have difficulty sustaining the exercise. Modifications to exercises can help accommodate that so everyone participates (e.g. perform push-ups with knees down) Students can also perform mini movements (e.g. only go halfway down in a lunge.)

HANDS OFF!

Calisthenics 3

Students take turns drawing cards from a deck. Each card has a specific joint movement. The students must select a repetitive full body movement activity (calisthenics or similar) that includes that joint movement. They perform their selection and keep going until the rest of the class successfully guesses what joint movement was on the card.

Materials and Implementation

Students should wear clothing and footwear that permits movement. An exercise mat is needed.

Face-to-Face

This activity works well in face-to-face classes.

Online Synchronous

This can be easily executed with students using webcams. To keep the discussion organized, the instructor might need to have a single student analyze while another performs calisthenics.

There should be adequate space to move comfortably and view students from the camera's position.

Online Asynchronous

Students could be assigned an exercise that they film themselves demonstrating and describing. The videos can be uploaded to a folder for the class to compare and contrast in a written forum.

Topic Areas

Anatomy & physiology

Kinesiology

Learning Stage Adaptation Examples

Review

The class should attempt to describe all joint movements while the student volunteer performs the exercise. Once they say the correct movement, another student takes a turn and selects a different card.

Application

After the students successfully identify the joint movement, they review agonist and antagonist muscles involved in that movement.

Integration

Have the students propose a variation that changes a kinesiology concept (e.g. widen feet in an exercise for a larger base of support.)

Link a repetitive stress injury or injury pattern associated with this exercise with a massage technique or stretch.

Diversity Considerations

Until students are comfortable in the class, some may be reluctant to think on their feet in front of everyone. Novice students could consult with the instructor after they think of an exercise to perform.

Students who are not physically fit may be reluctant to serve as the demonstrator or may have difficulty sustaining the exercise. Modifications to exercises can be suggested by the instructor.

HANDS OFF!

Mime Time 1

This activity involves demonstration of everyday tasks using mimed movements. The instructor can prepare a deck of index cards with different everyday tasks. One at a time, students draw a card and then silently perform movements of that activity. They keep doing the mimed activity until the rest of the class successfully guesses what it is and then discuss the movements involved in performing that activity.

Materials and Implementation

Students should wear clothing and footwear that permits movement.

Face-to-Face

Prepared deck of index cards with a variety of everyday movements

This activity works well in face-to-face classes. It can also be funny if students get creative in how they mime.

Online Synchronous

This can be easily executed with students using webcams. The instructor would need to assign each student a task using chat so the other students cannot see what will be done.

There should be adequate space to move comfortably and view students from camera position.

Online Asynchronous

Students could prepare short videos of themselves. These could be shared to a discussion forum for other students in the class to analyze

Topic Areas

Anatomy & physiology

Kinesiology

Pathophysiology

Learning Stage Adaptation Examples

Review

Students are asked to describe basic movements that are being demonstrated and the joints/muscles involved. Examples: Walking up or down stairs, carrying groceries, stirring a pot on the stove, or putting on a sweater

Application

More complex movements are used, and the students are asked to connect the muscles, joints, and movements with concepts from kinesiology. Examples:

— Washing a window and planes of movement
— Cleaning the shower or tub and center of gravity
— Changing an automobile tire involves a combination of static and dynamic movements

Integration

Link the everyday task with disorders or conditions that might interfere with ability to perform it on a needed basis. Then review treatments or other interventions that might help attenuate limitations or symptoms of a disorder or condition.

— Unloading the dishwasher and degenerative disk disease
— Planting flowers in a garden and hip replacement surgery
— Putting on pants and a vestibular disorder

Diversity Considerations

The concept of everyday activities differs among cultures and socioeconomic groups. The activities and movements selected for this strategy should reflect the general characteristics of the community so that they will be familiar for the students. Gardening, dishwashing, and changing an automobile's tire might not be familiar to all students.

Mime Time 2

This activity involves demonstration of everyday tasks using mimed movements. In this version, all students are given the same everyday task and need to mime the task at the same time. Time the miming for one full minute so that students engage in the activity in a way similar to real life. After the time is up, have the class compare and contrast differences in the ways they moved, how they felt muscles and joints working, and factors that influenced the movements.

Materials and Implementation

Students should wear clothing and footwear that permits movement.

Face-to-Face

Prepared list with a variety of everyday movements.

This activity works well in face-to-face classes. It can be fun to see different interpretations of normal everyday activities.

Online Synchronous

This could be difficult if all students are moving at the same time. Sight lines may be a problem. This could be modified to have students demonstrate in pairs or trios with the rest of the class observing.

Online Asynchronous

Students could prepare short videos of themselves. These could be shared to a discussion forum for other students in the class to analyze

Topic Areas

Anatomy & physiology

Kinesiology

KINESTHETIC ACTIVITIES

Learning Stage Adaptation Examples

Review

Observe differences in the movement patterns demonstrated by the class and reflect on how that demonstrates variation in muscle groups involved. Examples:
— Hailing a taxi
— Putting on a cardigan sweater
— Taking a shower

Application

Observe differences in the movement patterns demonstrated by the class and detail variations in activation of different agonist/antagonist muscles. Examples:
— Unpacking a suitcase
— Dusting a bookcase
— Raking leaves

Integration

Observe differences in the movement patterns demonstrated by the class, then discuss diseases or disorders that might contribute to different movement patterns.
— Putting on socks and shoes
— Building a model airplane
— Planting a tree

Diversity Considerations

The concept of everyday activity differs among cultures and socioeconomic groups. The activities and movements selected for this strategy should reflect the general characteristics of the community so that they will be familiar for the students. Hailing a taxi or raking leaves might not be familiar to all students.

HANDS OFF!

Mirror, Mirror 1

Organize students in pairs. They will alternate roles as "Mover" and "Mirror." Students should stand a few feet apart, facing each other, with room to allow movement. Each pair should decide who will move first. The instructor signals the start of the activity. The Mover slowly makes movements that the Mirror must mimic to make it seem that the Mover is looking in a mirror. After a few moments, the instructor says to switch roles, so the student who had been the Mover becomes the Mirror and has to follow the movement. The instructor can have students switch roles several times during this activity.

Materials and Implementation
Students should wear clothing and footwear that permits movement.

Face-to-Face

This activity works well in face-to-face classes. It can be funny, so it is a good stress-reliever.

Online Synchronous

This could work online, but only if one pair of students participates at a time. Sight lines may be a problem. If students demonstrate in pairs or trios, the rest of the class could observe and analyze motor skills.

Online Asynchronous

--

Topic Areas
Anatomy & physiology
Kinesiology

KINESTHETIC ACTIVITIES

Learning Stage Adaptation Examples

Review

The instructor asks the class to "freeze" in a position. Then both students hold that position for analysis:
- Joint positions
- Muscle agonist and antagonist activation
- Planes of motion

Application

The instructor asks the class to "freeze" in a position. Then both students hold that position and reflect on how it feels different when they are the mover compared to the mirror.

During the exercise, the mover attempts to challenge differences in balance, base of support, and center of gravity.

Integration

Either when students are instructed to "freeze," or after they participate in a series of movements, they are asked to identify diseases or disorders that might potentially interfere with abilities to perform the same movements.

Diversity Considerations

Some students may feel uncomfortable trying to mimic others—even if it is only movements. If that occurs, recognizing it and working to find solutions will help everyone to participate.

HANDS OFF!

Mirror, Mirror 2

Organize students in pairs. Designate one as the "Mover" and the other the "Mirror." Students should stand a few feet apart, facing each other, with room to allow movement. The instructor gives the Mover group an occupation or sport. At the start of the activity, the Mover slowly demonstrates movements associated with the occupation or activity. The Mirror must mimic these movements to make it seem that the Mover is looking in a mirror. After several minutes, end the activity and have students review their experience as Mover and Mirror. Then the students switch roles and are given a new sport or occupation to demonstrate.

Materials and Implementation

Students should wear clothing and footwear that permits movement.

Face-to-Face

This activity works well in face-to-face classes. It can be funny, so it is a good stress-reliever, especially if unusual sports or occupations are incorporated.

Online Synchronous

This could work online, but only if one pair of students participates at a time. Sight lines may be a problem. If students demonstrate in pairs or trios the rest of the class could observe and analyze motor skills.

Online Asynchronous

--

Topic Areas

Anatomy & physiology

Kinesiology

KINESTHETIC ACTIVITIES

Learning Stage Adaptation Examples

Review

Students reflect on joints and muscles involved in producing movements.

Students analyze different planes of motion involved in performance of a sport or tasks related to an occupation.

Application

Students are asked to describe how various positions challenged their balance, altered their base of support, or changed their center of gravity.

Integration

Students are asked to identify how the movements are related to risk of injury associated with the sport or occupation.

If students are unfamiliar with a sport or occupation, have the class suggest questions that could be incorporated into a client interview to help provide more information.

Have the students identify and review quality resources that provide information about the sport, including training, injuries, and recovery.

Diversity Considerations

Some students may feel uncomfortable trying to mimic others—even if it is only movements. If that occurs, recognizing it and working to find solutions will help everyone to participate.

Students may not be familiar with some sports or occupations. If that happens, instruct students to do their best during the activity then take time for class reflection afterwards.

Puppet Master

The students pair up and stand facing each other. One person is the "Master" and the other is the "Puppet." Each Master gives verbal instructions for the Puppet to perform a movement, or sequence of movements. The Master should use movement terminology and is not allowed to demonstrate anything. The Puppet can be scored on ability to execute the exact movements as dictated.

Materials and Implementation

Students should wear clothing and footwear that permits movement.

An exercise mat may be needed.

Face-to-Face

This activity works well as a quick review in lessons on joint actions, muscle origins/insertions/actions.

Online Synchronous

This could work online, but only if one pair of students participates at a time. Sight lines may be a problem. If students demonstrate in pairs or trios the rest of the class could observe and vote on whether the Puppet performed the correct movement.

Online Asynchronous

--

Topic Areas

Anatomy & physiology

Kinesiology

Pathophysiology

Clinical reasoning

KINESTHETIC ACTIVITIES

<u>Learning Stage Adaptation Examples</u>
Review
Use a deck of flash cards as students are learning muscle origins, insertions, and actions.
- Incorporate this activity as different areas of the body are introduced to give students a rapid review and build confidence (e.g. direct all movements of the hip joint.)
- At the end of muscle anatomy, have the Master draw several cards and try to direct the Puppet into a complex movement (e.g. flex the cervical spine, abduct the shoulder, and laterally rotate the hip.)

Application
After the puppet has executed a movement—or series of movements, the student pair can review muscles that act to produce the movement, as well as the innervation and blood supply for those muscles.

Integration
Students can brainstorm what disorders or conditions would make it difficult for a person to perform the movement (or series of movements.)

<u>Diversity Considerations</u>
This activity requires students to think on their feet. For slower learners it may be stressful if they have trouble making the connections between instructions and movement execution. Allowing pairs of students to work at their own pace can help everyone get something out of the activity.

Silly Walks

Gait observation is a useful assessment. It can be made more fun and challenging by adding some variety borrowed from *Monty Python's Flying Circus:* "The Ministry of Silly Walks."

Have students take turns as the subject of a gait assessment while performing a silly walk. Students can work in small groups to analyze the gait and describe ways that it deviates from a typical gait.

Materials and Implementation

Students should wear clothing and footwear that permits movement.

Face-to-Face

Students take turns performing a typical gait followed by a silly walk for the rest of the class to analyze.

Online Synchronous

--

Online Asynchronous

Students can be assigned to watch short YouTube clips from the *Monty Python* show and analyze the silly walk gait.

Topic Areas

Anatomy & physiology

Kinesiology

Learning Stage Adaptation Examples

Review

Describe bilateral joint movements that are used in the silly walk.

Identify agonist muscles acting to produce the movements.

Application

Discuss the role of stabilizer muscles in producing the silly walk movements.

Analyze how center of gravity shifts with the silly walk movements compared to a typical gait.

Integration

Compare biomechanics concepts when the same silly walk is performed at different speeds (e.g. a slower speed involves less momentum which changes muscle activation compared to a faster speed.)

Diversity Considerations

Some students may not be familiar with *Monty Python's Flying Circus* or the humor associated with the program. Context may be helpful.

Some students may feel uncomfortable being the center of attention. If that occurs, recognizing it and working to find solutions will help everyone to participate.

Strong or Flexible

This activity encourages students to explore factors affecting muscle tonus and joint range of motion. A deck of index cards is prepared that lists titles for different occupations or recreational activity (e.g. firefighter, linebacker, golfer) There should be one card for each student in the class. Have students stand in a straight line. Give each student a card from the deck. That is their assigned "role." Then the students must work collaboratively to position themselves in a line organized from strongest to most flexible. After the students agree on their final line, they need to defend the arrangement of their line based upon their understanding of the different roles.

Materials and Implementation

Prepared deck of index cards with enough roles for the entire class.

Face-to-Face

The entire class can participate as a single group or the activity can have several groups of students.

Online Synchronous

Student roles could be virtually assigned. Then the class could use a wiki or a shared document to edit the order of the roles.

Online Asynchronous

This works well using a wiki. But instead of assigning students to individual roles, each student could be required to insert two new roles somewhere on the order of a list.

Topic Areas

Kinesiology

Clinical reasoning

KINESTHETIC ACTIVITIES

Learning Stage Adaptation Examples

Review

Recognize different factors that affect joint range of motion.

Application

Identify activities related to performing the role that can affect posture and range of motion.

Integration

After the class has finished the activity, ask students to describe how active and passive range of motion assessment would potentially differ across the various roles.

Diversity Considerations

This activity requires collaboration and cooperation. Some students may feel uncomfortable voicing opinions that differ from others in the class. Gently encouraging all students to participate can help foster negotiation skills.

Select roles for the activity reflect industries in the surrounding community (e.g. jobs in manufacturing, farming, fishing, finance) to help students make connections.

Observational Activities

HANDS OFF!

Sports Stars 1

Gather photos of athletes in action. Assign different photos to small groups of students. Have them analyze the position of the athlete and identify where the position in the photo occurs in a movement sequence used in the sport. After the students have worked in small groups, have each group present their findings and analysis to the class.

Materials and Implementation

A selection of photos from magazines or websites.

Face-to-Face

This activity works well to facilitate review and give students the opportunity to present to each other.

Online Synchronous

This can work well in an online session by displaying photos online for analysis.

Online Asynchronous

A discussion forum with a thread for each photo that allows students to describe the position. They could also create short videos that display where the photo is in a movement sequence.

Topic Areas

Kinesiology

Pathophysiology

Clinical reasoning

OBSERVATIONAL ACTIVITIES

Learning Stage Adaptation Examples

Review

Describe how the base of support and center of gravity change through the movement sequence.

Application

Relate the position of the athlete to the sport and describe antecedent and subsequent movements related to the position.

Integration

If students are unfamiliar with a sport or occupation, have the class suggest questions that could be incorporated into a client interview to help provide more information.

Have the students identify and review quality resources that provide information about the sport including training, injuries, and recovery and relate that information to the position in the photo.

List tests they could use to assess passive or active insufficiencies associated with the movement in the picture (or the sport in general.)

Diversity Considerations

Students may not be familiar with some sports or occupations. If that happens, instruct students to do their best during the activity then take time for class reflection afterwards.

HANDS OFF!

Sports Stars 2

This activity helps students make connections to repetitive movements used in a single sport. Choose one sport and have students take turns standing in front of the class and demonstrate a movement sequence used in the sport. Have the student perform a few times and then freeze in the middle of the movement sequence. When the student is "frozen" in position, the class can analyze the position. Examples from tennis: serve, forehand, single backhand, double backhand.

After one movement sequence has been analyzed, invite another student to demonstrate a different sports movement sequence. To encourage students to recognize different movement patterns associated with team sports, have them perform different roles. Examples from baseball: pitcher, catcher, or umpire.

Materials and Implementation

Students should wear clothing and footwear that permits movement.

Face-to-Face

This activity can work well in class provided students are familiar with the sport being demonstrated.

Online Synchronous

This could work online with students demonstrating movements on webcam. Sight lines may be a problem.

Online Asynchronous

A discussion forum could prompt students to compare and contrast photos of two different positions from a sport or two different roles.

Topic Areas

Kinesiology

Clinical reasoning

Learning Stage Adaptation Examples

Review

Students compare and contrast how the same muscles are used differently in movements for a single sport.

Review base of support and center of gravity associated with the movement and movement sequence.

Application

Have the student who is demonstrating reflect on the muscles used through the whole movement sequence.

Integration

Students are asked to identify how the movements are related to risk of injury associated with the sport or occupation.

Ask the students to find a training or recovery recommendation for the sport, relate it to the movement, and analyze research evidence supporting effectiveness.

Invite students debate the pros and cons of returning to play when recovering from a repetitive injury in the sport.

Diversity Considerations

Some students may feel uncomfortable being the center of attention. If that occurs, recognizing it and working to find solutions will help everyone to participate.

Students may not be familiar with some sports or occupations. If that happens, instruct students to do their best during the activity then take time for class reflection afterwards.

Sports Stars 3

This activity helps students analyze complex movements, kinetic chains, and movement sequences. Find video clips of athletes in motion. Start with one video and watch it with students. Replay the video several times to allow students to document and analyze the movements. Then, use different videos from the same sport or a different sport to give students the opportunity to repeat the activity several times.

Materials and Implementation

Access to a video library.

Face-to-Face

A computer and projector are needed. Students can work individually or in small groups. If small groups are used this can be a team-based learning activity when the groups compare and contrast their findings.

Online Synchronous

This could work online with the whole class or small groups reviewing videos.

Online Asynchronous

A discussion forum with a thread for each video would allow students to work individually or in small groups.

Topic Areas

Anatomy & physiology

Kinesiology

Pathophysiology

Clinical reasoning

OBSERVATIONAL ACTIVITIES

Learning Stage Adaptation Examples

Review

Identify kinetic chains.

Review base of support and center of gravity associated with the movement and movement sequence.

Summarize primary muscle groups that produce movements.

Application

Relate the position of the athlete to the sport and describe antecedent and subsequent movements related to the position.

Integration

If students are unfamiliar with a sport or occupation, have the class suggest questions that could be incorporated into a client interview to help provide more information.

Have the students identify and review quality resources that provide information about the sport including training, injuries, and recovery and relate that information to the position in the photo.

List tests they could use to assess passive or active insufficiencies associated with the movement in the picture, or the sport in general.

Diversity Considerations

This activity presents an opportunity to introduce students to a wide range of sports. Snowboarding, platform diving, and gymnastics are not necessarily the types of sports they will encounter in their practice, but these sports provide excellent opportunities for review and analysis.

Dancers 1

This activity helps students analyze similarities and differences in body position and movement. Look online for photos of different ballet or modern dancers. Find pairs of photos of different dancers performing the same movement. There are variations in pirouette, arabesque, attitude, développé, etc. Students can work individually or in small groups to compare and contrast differences between the dancers.

Materials and Implementation

Photos of dancers are needed for this activity.

Face-to-Face

A computer and projector are needed. Students can work individually or in small groups. If small groups are used this can be a team-based learning activity when the groups defend their findings.

Online Synchronous

This could work if the pictures are shown online and students take turns contributing to the analysis. Small groups could also be used with students preparing a summary and then presenting it to the class.

Online Asynchronous

This may work as an assignment if students are asked to individually analyze different pairs of photos and then post their responses to a discussion forum for the remainder of the class to review.

Topic Areas

Anatomy & physiology

Kinesiology

Pathophysiology

Clinical reasoning

OBSERVATIONAL ACTIVITIES

Learning Stage Adaptation Examples

Review

Analyze joint positions.

Reflect on biomechanics concepts.

Go over muscle group activation and potential variations.

Application

Explore how antecedent and subsequent movements related to the positions might differ.

Identify active and passive insufficiencies that might contribute to inability for dancers to perform the same movement.

Integration

Identify how the movements are related to risk of injury associated with the form of dance demonstrated.

Design interview questions for dancers to gather information to design a treatment.

Diversity Considerations

Ballet works well for this activity because there is consistency to the position terminology and choreography. However, all students may not be familiar with ballet. Scaffolding the activity can provide an introduction. Review terminology for the body position, introduce a dance position, and then review photographs of different dancers in the same position. To recognize diversity in dance, look for photos of other dance forms. Have students learn the associated terminology and then review body positions.

Dancers 2

Comparing different styles of dance can help students gain insight into the varying demands placed on a dancer's body. Look for short video clips of different dance styles. Play one video clip a few times for students to analyze. Then, play another video clip from a different dance style. After the students have analyzed both video clips, invite them to compare and contrast how different dancers use their bodies.

Materials and Implementation

Access to a video library.

Face-to-Face

A computer and projector are needed. Students can work individually or in small groups to conduct their analysis and then discuss their findings.

Online Synchronous

This could work using small groups and different videos for each group. Students would work in breakout rooms to conduct their analysis. Then their videos could be played for the class and they can present their findings.

Online Asynchronous

This could work as an assignment that required students to individually respond to the videos.

A discussion forum could also be used to ask students to post individual observations that are different from others already posted by other students.

Topic Areas

Kinesiology

Pathophysiology

Clinical reasoning

OBSERVATIONAL ACTIVITIES

Learning Stage Adaptation Examples
Review
Analyze variations in joint positions and muscle activation.
Contrast differences in muscle groups involved in the different dance forms.
Application
Review biomechanics concepts relative to the different choreography.
Integration
Identify how injury patterns would likely be different in the two dance styles.
Design interview questions that could be used to gather information from dancers about their participation in different dance styles and how that might contribute to injury risk.

Diversity Considerations

Because this activity involves different dance styles, it offers the opportunity to include dance from different cultures. Students could contribute to the assignment by finding video clips that can be used in class.

Musicians 1

Playing a musical instrument involves repetitive movements. This activity helps students recognize how musicians use joints and muscle groups. It also provides an opportunity to review risks associated with—and treatment options for—repetitive stress injuries.

Find short video clips of musicians playing and have students analyze posture and movements. The clips can be of a single musician, or two different musicians to compare variations in posture and movements. Students can review the videos several times to give adequate time to document the movements for analysis. Then then their videos could be played for the class and they can present their findings.

Materials and Implementation

Access to a video library is needed.

Face-to-Face

A computer and projector are needed. Students can work individually or in small groups to conduct their analysis and then discuss their findings.

Online Synchronous

Students can work individually or in small groups in breakout rooms to conduct their analyses.

Online Asynchronous

This could work as an assignment that required students to individually respond to the videos.

A discussion forum could also be used to ask students to post individual observations that are different from posts by other students.

Topic Areas

Pathophysiology

Clinical reasoning

OBSERVATIONAL ACTIVITIES

Learning Stage Adaptation Examples

Review

Identify muscles used in producing movements and review innervation pathways.

Application

List risk factors associated with repetitive stress injuries and relate those risks to the movement patterns seen in the videos.

Integration

Identify factors that might contribute to different injury patterns among different individuals playing the same musical instrument

Design interview questions that could be used to gather information from musicians about instrument and how that might contribute to injury risk.

Have the students identify and review quality resources that provide information about musculoskeletal problems associated with the instrument and how they are treated.

Diversity Considerations

This activity offers a chance to look at musical instruments that might be played by clients in the community and also at instruments from different cultures.

The types of movements used to play different musical instruments and practice routines are associated with injury risk. Movements of the fingers for woodwinds, arm movements when playing percussion, and the unilateral motor skills used for string instruments contribute to a variety of different injury risks.

Musicians 2

This activity helps students recognize how music making involves repetitive movements that are different for various instruments. Find short video clips of musicians playing different instruments in a group (e.g. popular bands, orchestras, concerts or marching bands.) View the videos with the students several times asking them to focus on different players each time. Then compare and contrast similarities and differences they observe.

Materials and Implementation

Access to a video library.

Face-to-Face

A computer and projector are needed. Students can work individually or in small groups to conduct their analysis and then discuss their findings.

Online Synchronous

Students can work individually or in small groups in breakout rooms to conduct their analyses. Then then their videos could be played for the class and they can present their findings.

Online Asynchronous

This could work as an assignment that required students to individually respond to the videos.

A discussion forum could also be used to ask students to post individual observations that are different from others already posted by other students.

Topic Areas

Pathophysiology

Clinical reasoning

Learning Stage Adaptation Examples

Review

Compare and contrast different joint movements and muscles.

Application

Identify different risk factors related to the movement patterns observed.

Integration

Design interview questions that could be used to gather information from musicians about their instrument and how that might contribute to injury risk.

Have the students identify and review quality resources that provide information about musculoskeletal problems associated with different instruments and how they are treated.

Diversity Considerations

This activity offers a chance to look at musical instruments that might be played by clients in the community and also at instruments from different cultures.

The types of movements used to play different musical instruments and practice routines are associated with injury risk. Movements of the fingers for woodwinds, arm movements when playing percussion, and the unilateral motor skills used for string instruments contribute to a variety of different injury risks.

HANDS OFF!

Famous Statues

Statues provide excellent opportunities to study the human form, joint position, muscular definition and posture, They can be helpful in kinesiology to have students understand different ways base of support and center of gravity affect posture and balance. Viewing statues from different countries and cultures can be a fun and interesting learning experience.

Find a collection of photographs of famous—or not so famous—statues. Assign different photos to small groups of students. Have them analyze the posture working from head-to-toe or toe-to-head. After the students have worked in small groups, have each group present their findings and analysis to the class.

Materials and Implementation

Access to a search engine to find pictures of statues is needed.

Face-to-Face

This activity works well in a face-to-face setting.

Online Synchronous

This could work using breakout rooms followed by the presentation of findings to the class.

Online Asynchronous

This might work adapted as an individual assignment. Each student could be assigned a photo for analysis. The findings could be posted in a discussion forum for other students and the instructor to ask follow-up questions.

Topic Areas

Kinesiology

Clinical reasoning

OBSERVATIONAL ACTIVITIES

Learning Stage Adaptation Examples

Review

Review joint positions and associated muscle activity.

Identify position of joints in relation to movement planes.

Application

Compare difference between active insufficiency and passive insufficiency needed to achieve joint range of motion.

Review biomechanics concepts relative to the position (e.g. base of support, center of gravity.)

Integration

--

Diversity Considerations

In some cultures, statues are used to display nationalist or spiritual ideal. Care should be taken in facilitating the discussion to honor that for all cultures.

This activity could present an opportunity to discuss how statues are crafted to convey different emotions and characteristics of the subject.

HANDS OFF!

Fashion Models 1

Gather some magazines or catalogues with pictures of people modeling clothing or accessories. Students use the photo of the model to review and analyze the position of the body.

This can be done as a speed activity requiring students to list as many joint positions as they can in one minute. This is a nice activity to help students develop a systematic approach to analyzing posture.

This activity can be used as a low-stakes assessment.

Materials and Implementation

A selection of magazines or catalogues.

Face-to-Face

A selection of different photos can be used and passed around to the class. All students write an analysis of each photo. Afterwards, the students can compare different answers.

Online Synchronous

A series of photos can be used and shown to the whole class at once so each student can write an analysis. Afterward the class can compare and contrast different answers.

Online Asynchronous

Students can be assigned photos to analyze and submit individual answer sheets.

Topic Areas

Anatomy & physiology

Kinesiology

Pathophysiology

Clinical reasoning

Learning Stage Adaptation Examples

Review

Identify position of joints in relation to movement planes.

Describe positions of as many joints as they can within the time frame. Repetition of this activity can be used to help them create a systematic approach to postural analysis.

After identifying the position of a joint, students identify agonist muscles that used to execute that movement.

Application

Review biomechanics concepts relative to the position (e.g. base of support, center of gravity.)

Integration

List active or passive insufficiencies that might make it difficult for someone else to assume the same position.

Discuss how to incorporate postural assessment into intake for a new client.

Diversity Considerations

Among cultural groups that value modesty, pictures of scantily clad individuals may be offensive. To help all students feel comfortable, the magazines or catalogues used should have pictures of models that are clothed (i.e. not shirtless, wearing lingerie, or a bathing suit.)

Fashion Models 2

Gather some magazines or catalogues with pictures of people modeling clothing or accessories. Have students pair up. One student ("Instructor") randomly selects a page with a picture of a model. Then the Instructor guides the "Model" to assume the same position as the picture by detailing the position of each joint from head-to-toe—or toe-to-head.

Once the Model has assumed the position, he or she gets to view the picture to assess whether or not they've succeeded.

For an added challenge, the Instructor student is not allowed to make any corrections. If/when the Model does not assume the right position (e.g. medially rotates hip instead of performing lateral rotation) the Instructor moves on to focus on other joints. This can be very funny when the Model finally gets to see the picture.

Materials and Implementation

A selection of magazines or catalogues.

Face-to-Face

This activity works well to help students become familiar with describing and listening to anatomical terminology.

Online Synchronous

This could be difficult if all students were moving at the same time. Sight lines may be a problem. This could be modified to have students demonstrate in pairs or trios with the rest of the class observing.

Online Asynchronous

--

Topic Areas
Anatomy & physiology
Kinesiology

Learning Stage Adaptation Examples

Review

Practice describing joint positions, trying to execute them, and getting a picture to help them identify whether or not they were successful.

Application

After the Model has achieved the same position in the picture, he or she outlines the muscles or muscle groups that produce the joint movements.

Integration

--

Diversity Considerations

Among cultural groups that value modesty, pictures of scantily-clad individuals may be offensive. To help all students feel comfortable, the magazines or catalogues used should have pictures of models that are clothed (i.e. not shirtless, wearing lingerie, or a bathing suit.)

This activity requires students to think on their feet. For slower learners, it may be stressful if they have trouble making the connections between instructions and movement execution. Allowing pairs of students to work at their own pace can help everyone get something out of the activity.

What am I?

Study of diseases and disorders can be very dry. Instead of trying to diagnose a condition related to a person, the students need to discern characteristics of a disease or disorder. The instructor prepares narratives: a few sentences written in first person that describes a disease or disorder through various clues. The narratives are read aloud, and students write down what is being described. This can be followed by a class discussion to review answers. This activity helps promote listening skills. It also works well as a low-stakes assessment.

Materials and Implementation

A previously prepared series of cases sheets for students.

Face-to-Face

The narratives can be read aloud. After all are read and answered the class can discuss their answers and provide rationale.

Online Synchronous

This could work with a modification to ensure academic integrity if this activity is used as an assessment. Students would need to submit their answers before any discussion took place.

Online Asynchronous

This could be formatted as a quiz using recorded audio readings of the narratives.

Topic Areas

Pathophysiology

Clinical reasoning

Learning Stage Adaptation Examples

Review

Students work through ways to identify relevant information and keywords (underlined below in the example for ankle sprain.)

— "I am a common <u>injury</u> in <u>sports</u> that involve running and jumping. <u>Tripping</u> or <u>stumbling</u> can <u>overextend the joint.</u> This stimulates intrafusal muscle fibers (<u>muscle spindles</u>) to <u>suddenly and forcefully contract</u>."

Application

Combining information about assessments that could be performed prior to designing a massage treatment promotes critical thinking. An example for nonspecific low back pain:

— "The test for Lasègue's sign can be useful to distinguish me from lumbar radiculopathy, disc protrusion, or degenerative disc disease."

Integration

Linking the narrative to anticipated outcomes from massage helps to reinforce the difference between direct and indirect effects of massage. An example for type 2 diabetes:

— "I am a metabolic disease. Chronic hyperglycemia caused by insulin resistance can lead to neuropathy, blindness, or renal disease. I can be managed with a combination of diet, exercise, and blood glucose monitoring."

Diversity Considerations

English-language learners and students who receive testing accommodations may have difficulty. The narratives should be read slowly and clearly. If this activity is used for an assessment, remediation may be warranted to ensure that all students have adequate learning opportunity.

HANDS OFF!

Dolly and Me

For students who struggle with anatomy and physiology, this offers a creative way to review and can help retain information. For this activity, students are asked to bring a doll or stuffed animal to class. It should be human-shaped (head, torso, arms, legs) and large enough to identify different areas of the body with some specificity. As the instructor describes anatomical structures (e.g. muscles, nerves, blood vessels, or organs) the students palpate on their doll or stuffed animal to demonstrate they know the location.

This activity can be interesting when students work with different types of dolls or stuffed animals. It can be challenging because students will need to approximate where structures are located on dolls or stuffed animals that lack palpable landmarks (e.g. a teddy bear does not have a scapula so the student would need to approximate its location.) This requires more scrutiny by the students.

Materials and Implementation

A human-shaped doll or stuffed animal for the instructor and every student.

Face-to-Face

This activity works well for a face-to-face class. The instructor can easily see when students have made accurate identifications.

Online Synchronous

Webcam required. Students could demonstrate by holding their doll or stuffed animal up to the webcam.

Online Asynchronous

--

Topic Areas

Anatomy & physiology

Pathophysiology

OBSERVATIONAL ACTIVITIES

Learning Stage Adaptation Examples

Review

Trace origins and insertions of muscles

Identify bony landmarks

Identify location of major organs

Application

Give students origins and insertions then ask them to identify the muscle.

Start with a landmark (e.g. greater trochanter, ischial tuberosity) and ask students to trace all muscles associated with that landmark.

Integration

Ask students to connect relevant anatomical structures with diseases or disorders and then describe a brief and specific treatment plan (e.g. ankle sprain, thoracic outlet syndrome, rotator cuff injury.)

Diversity Considerations

Some students may not have, or be able to afford to buy, a doll or stuffed animal. To help these students feel included, planning ahead is important. Students may need to find a way to borrow one so they can participate in the activity.

Dolls and stuffed animals have cultural connections and often have deep personal significance. This can provide an interesting topic for discussion. As an icebreaker, students could introduce their doll or stuffed animal to the class.

HANDS OFF!

One-Minute Paper

Start class with a blank piece of paper. For one full minute, students write a narrative. They must keep writing until the minute is up. Students can turn in their papers to give informal feedback to the instructor. The papers an also be used to stimulate class discussion. Students can be asked to summarize the essence of what they wrote. They can form small groups to share what they wrote with each other. Then each group can report back to the class about similarities and differences. This can be especially useful at a stressful time in the course when it can be helpful to know if—and how—students are struggling. The One-Minute-Paper can also be used as a self-reflection by asking students to write about what they have learned.

Materials and Implementation

Blank paper and pen/pencil

Face-to-Face

This activity works well as an icebreaker to promote class discussion.

Online Synchronous

Students can complete a timed writing assignment before the class session and then discuss their writings during an open forum in class.

Online Asynchronous

This can be a timed writing assignment submitted to the instructor for a no-stakes assessment.

Topic Areas

Anatomy & physiology

Kinesiology

Pathophysiology

Ethics

Learning Stage Adaptation Examples

Review

This is an excellent review activity to help students reflect on what they have learned or describe where they are struggling. Potential topics include:

— One concept I understand very well...
— Something I am confused about...
— What we learned in our last class...

Application

This activity can help students recognize how well they are drawing upon foundational material. Potential topics include:

— What information from another course has been most useful in this class?
— What does professionalism mean to me?

Integration

This activity can help students recognize how they are using critical thinking skills. Potential topics include:

— What would I do with a client who has a medical diagnosis I have never heard of before?
— How well do I feel I can incorporate assessments into a session?

Diversity Considerations

This is a good opportunity to hear from students who are reluctant to speak up in class.

If papers will be read aloud in class or shared among the students, let everyone know before the activity begins. Students have a right to privacy and should be informed ahead of time how the information they write will be used and shared (if applicable.)

Collaborative Activities

Daisy Chain

A daisy chain is a string of flowers woven together by their stems that can be worn as a hat or necklace. The concept of threading something together can be used in a learning activity by asking students to connect ideas in a sequence to design a massage treatment. Present a case scenario to the class. Take time for some questions and answers so students can come up with ideas for a treatment design. Start at one side of the classroom with a blank piece of paper. Have that student write how they would start the massage. Then the paper is passed to the next student who "continues" the massage by writing what they would do next. Then the paper is passed to the next student and so on until either: (a) it reaches the end of the class, or (b) the treatment is concluded. Follow up with a class discussion about the treatment design and how it relates to the case scenario.

Materials and Implementation

A prepared case scenario using narrative or an intake form to provide pre-treatment information. Blank paper and pen/pencil

Face-to-Face

The paper can easily be passed around the class. Keeping students on task and engaged in the activity may be challenging if circulation of the paper stalls.

Online Synchronous

This could be modified to use one "treatment" at a time with a collaborative document.

Online Asynchronous

This could work in collaborative documents with follow up in a discussion forum.

Topic Areas

Pathophysiology

Clinical reasoning

Learning Stage Adaptation Examples

Review

Structure the case scenario with information that references material in a specific course unit. Examples:
- A client with osteopenia
- A post marathon massage for an elite runner
- A client with relapsing-remitting multiple sclerosis

Application

Present a more complex case scenario that requires clinical reasoning skills. Examples:
- A client with osteopenia and chronic back pain
- A post-marathon massage for an elite runner who reports thigh pain
- A client with relapsing-remitting multiple sclerosis who wants a relaxation massage

Integration

Use a complex case and ask the students to include assessments. Examples:
- A client with osteopenia and chronic back pain with limited trunk rotation
- A post-marathon massage for an elite runner who has radiating pain down the posterior right thigh
- A client with relapsing-remitting multiple sclerosis who is having exacerbated symptoms

Diversity Considerations

This activity requires contributions from each student in the class. It is a nice way to balance students who are reluctant to speak up in class with overeager students who can dominate discussions.

Minus One, Plus One

This is a collaborative activity to help students see how a treatment can be modified. Prepare sheets of paper prepared with a 3-4 column grid; the number of columns should equal the number of students in the group. The instructor presents a case scenario. Each group begins with every student writing a treatment sequence in the first column, then the papers are passed to another student in the group. The next student replaces one part of the treatment with a different technique by writing a different technique in the second column. The papers are passed again, and the next student replaces a different technique from the first column with a new one. After all columns are used, the paper is returned to the originator. Each student in the group will have their original treatment with modifications suggested by the other students. The students take turns reviewing the substituted information.

Materials and Implementation

A prepared case scenario using narrative.

Sheets of paper prepared with grids.

Face-to-Face

This activity works well to engage students in small groups.

Online Synchronous

This could be done with collaborative documents and breakout rooms.

Online Asynchronous

This could work in collaborative documents with follow up in a discussion forum.

Topic Areas

Clinical reasoning

COLLABORATIVE ACTIVITIES

Learning Stage Adaptation Examples

Review

Schedule the activity so students can review techniques learned in recent hands-on classes. Example:
— When students can perform different types of full-body relaxation massages

Application

Schedule this activity after students have completed a specific module or course section. Examples:
— Different techniques to treat rotator cuff injuries
— Different approaches for a client with chronic nonspecific low back pain

Integration

Schedule this activity after students have completed several techniques courses and use case scenarios that could be treated with different combinations of techniques. Examples:
— General massage, trigger point therapy, myofascial release, and/or stretching for hamstring strain
— Swedish massage and Shiatsu techniques in combination for tension type headaches

Diversity Considerations

This activity requires students to think on their feet. Slower learners may feel stressed if they need more time than others in their group. Encouraging the groups to work collaboratively can help.

This activity requires students to provide rationale for their selection of treatment techniques Students who are reluctant to speak up in class may feel uncomfortable defending their choices to their colleagues. Remind students that massage treatment designs are individualized so all ideas should be considered.

HANDS OFF!

Rowing Team

Students arrange themselves like rowing teams by sitting 3 or 4 to a row. In each row, all students except one sit facing the back of the room. The remaining student is the coxswain, and sits facing the front of the room—and their team. To begin, the instructor shows a term or concept to the coxswains. Each coxswain selects a related term or concept and writes it on a sheet of paper and hands it to the next student on their team. That student writes a different related term or concept on a new sheet of paper, and hands it to the student directly behind. This process repeats until reaching the last student. Each student only sees one term/concept in addition to their own as each team builds a terminology sequence. After all students have written a word, each "rowing team" takes turns holding up their list for the class to see. The class can compare and contrast how the terms relate to each other. Repeat this activity several times for different terms/concepts in an instructional unit.

Materials and Implementation

Blank paper, pen or pencil

A prepared list of terms or concepts for review.

Face-to-Face

This activity is designed for a face-to-face classroom with room to arrange students in rows. Students should write large enough for the whole class to see their answer.

Online Synchronous

--

Online Asynchronous

--

Topic Areas

Anatomy & physiology

Pathophysiology

COLLABORATIVE ACTIVITIES

Learning Stage Adaptation Examples

Review

Start with anatomy terms (e.g. bones, bony landmarks, muscles, nerves, etc.) to encourage students to recognize connections. For example, starting with "femur" could reveal answer sequences like:
— Hip, sacrum, lumbar spine, ribcage
— Quadriceps, patella, tibial tuberosity, fibula
— Long bone, humerus, acromioclavicular joint, scapula

Application

Start with physiology concepts to help students make connections to anatomy. For example, starting with "elasticity" could reveal answer sequences like:
— Contraction, Golgi tendon organ, load, recruitment
— Stretch, muscle spindle, reflex, interneuron
— Smooth muscle, blood circulation, valve, vein

Integration

Start with diseases or disorders to help students make connections that could inform treatment design. For example, starting with "heart disease" could reveal answer sequences like:
— Myocardial infarction, angina, coronary circulation, bypass
— Atherosclerosis, cholesterol, plaque, lipids
— Hypertension, diabetes, glucose, insulin

Diversity Considerations

This type of activity requires collaboration. This may be difficult for students who are used to working independently. Efforts to make the activity fun and engaging can help encourage reluctant students to work together.

Students who struggle to master concepts may benefit from seeing evidence of how other students make connections to material.

HANDS OFF!

Dominos

Dominos is a board game that involves laying numbered pieces end-to-end by matching the numbers on each piece. This vocabulary activity uses a similar concept to help students make connections by linking terms and definitions with each other.

This activity begins with one student selecting and defining a term. The next student must select a related term, describe the relationship, and share the definition of the term. The next student does the same and the activity circulates around so each student in the class contributes a term. As the activity moves across the class the definitions a dominos game because one term must in some way match the next.

The instructor can keep track of each term on a whiteboard or flipchart. After the whole class has made a contribution, they can review the list of collected terms and discuss the connections.

Materials and Implementation

Whiteboard or Flipchart.

A glossary of terms may be helpful.

Face-to-Face

This works well in a face-to-face class. Arranging chairs in rows or a semicircle can help to keep the activity flowing.

Online Synchronous

This could be adapted by having the students work in a collaborative document.

Online Asynchronous

--

Topic Areas

Pathophysiology

Ethics

Learning Stage Adaptation Examples

Review

This activity can be used to help students review terms and definitions, but guidance may be needed from the instructor to help students identify ways to make connections with new information. For example: the first student chooses "confidentiality" and the next student chooses "privacy," but the following student struggles to find a related term. The instructor might offer a scenario when confidentiality and privacy are needed to help the student think of a related term such as "interview," "HIPAA," or "documentation."

Application

This activity is an excellent reinforcement opportunity by using terms from the current as well as previous course units or modules. For example: the activity could ask the students to contribute terms from sessions on general healthcare ethics, sexual harassment, and documentation.

Integration

This activity can be adapted to foster critical thinking by asking the students to alternate a term from a didactic course with a term from a clinical course. For example: the first student defines "spasticity," the next student could define "stretch," and the next student could define "multiple sclerosis."

Diversity Considerations

This type of activity can be challenging for students who are reluctant to speak up in class. Encouraging the class to be respectful and listen carefully can help students feel more comfortable.

This may be difficult for slower learners and English-language learners. Asking other students to work as a partner by offering clues or ideas, or having students refer to a glossary to give clues can help everyone participate through a collaborative approach.

Connect the Dots

Mind maps are diagrams that are created to visually organize information. Creating a mind map helps students connect the dots by showing how terms or concepts are connected and interrelated through an arrangement of branches/nodes. This activity starts with a theme that is written in the middle of a blank page. Related terms or concepts are written in the area around the theme with lines (branches/nodes) drawn to connect terms/concepts to the central theme. Additional terms/concepts are added to expand the map into smaller branches that radiate outward from the central theme. Once completed a photo of the map can be shared with the class.

Materials and Implementation

Whiteboard and markers or a mind-mapping app projected from computer or tablet.

Face-to-Face

Students can take turns contributing a term/concept and making a connection to another term/concept on the board.

Online Synchronous

PowerPoint or a mind-mapping app could be used assigning one student to be the recorder, use a screen share with the class, and having the students take turns suggesting terms and connections.

Online Asynchronous

This could work in a collaborative document with students making contributions and corrections.

Topic Areas

Pathophysiology

Clinical reasoning

Ethics

COLLABORATIVE ACTIVITIES

Learning Stage Adaptation Examples

Review

This can be helpful for students to recognize, define, and label terms/concepts from a list from a course unit or module. Students can select a term/concept from the list, place it on the map, connect it to another term/concept and then provide rationale for their choice.

Application

This is an excellent activity to help students apply information from didactic and hands-on classes. It also can help students visualize complex conditions. Have students work individually or in small groups to construct mind maps on a single topic and then share with the class.

Integration

Students could work in several small groups collaborating on mind maps for different themes. Once completed the maps can be presented to the class for review. For example, if groups create mind maps for chronic fatigue syndrome, fibromyalgia, clinical depression, and complex regional pain syndrome this could create an opportunity to compare and contrast these conditions.

Diversity Considerations

For students who struggle with study skills, this activity can be helpful to show them a creative way to prepare a study guide on a complex topic.

This activity may be challenging for students who measure success by test scores. Using this as a low-stakes assessment can help to engage those students who may otherwise be reluctant to participate.

Strips in Sequence

Memorizing the steps in a process can be challenging. This psychomotor activity can help students retain information by engaging them through activity and collaboration.

Write steps in a process on strips of paper or index cards. Shuffle the strips and place them face down on a table. Have students work in small groups arrange the strips in the order of the process. Once the students have finished arranging their strips of paper, review and discuss their findings.

Materials and Implementation

Prepared strips of paper or index cards.

Face-to-Face

This activity is designed for a face-to-face classroom that has a large table or counter space for students to work.

Online Synchronous

This could be modified for an online class if students work in break out rooms and a collaborative slide to arrange blocks of prepared text.

Online Asynchronous

--

Topic Areas

Anatomy & physiology

Kinesiology

Pathophysiology

Clinical reasoning

COLLABORATIVE ACTIVITIES

<u>Learning Stage Adaptation Examples</u>
Review
This is a nice activity to include in anatomy & physiology review. Example topics:
- Order of blood circulation
- Kinetic chain associated with specific movements
- Reflex arc

Application
This activity could be helpful for students to refer to anatomy & physiology when learning about diseases or disorders. Example topics:
- Cardiac conduction pathway review when studying heart diseases
- Cell growth and proliferation when learning about cancer

Integration
--

<u>Diversity Considerations</u>
This activity may be easy for students with good memorization abilities and very challenging for students who struggle to memorize material. Encouraging all students to collaborate is important so everyone can get something out of the activity.

Plus or Minus

Assessment is both an art and a science. Recognizing variation in clinical presentation can help students differentiate between diseases and disorders that have similar presentation. This activity provides a nice opportunity for informal assessment. It can also be helpful for students to recognize how well they are mastering material.

Prepare a worksheet with a table that lists signs and symptoms in the first column and has several blank columns to the right. Present several case scenarios to the class. Ask students to write the scenario at the top of a column and then indicate in that column whether each sign or symptom would likely be present ("+") or absent ("-"). After students have recorded their answers for several scenarios, the class can review to compare, discuss, and defend their answers.

Materials and Implementation

Prepared worksheets. Pen or pencil.

Face-to-Face

This activity works well in a face-to-face class to encourage discussion during a review of a course unit or module.

Online Synchronous

An online version of this activity could be set up to have students submit their completed worksheets prior to any discussion.

Online Asynchronous

The cases could be presented using short recordings and students could submit their answers using a survey.

Topic Areas

Pathophysiology

Clinical reasoning

Learning Stage Adaptation Examples

Review

This type of activity is well suited to a review at the end of a course unit or module. For example, a unit on neuromuscular disorders might use case scenarios describing disorders such as whiplash, carpal tunnel syndrome, temporomandibular joint syndrome, and thoracic outlet syndrome.

Application

This type of activity is very helpful to encourage students to recognize characteristics of diseases and disorders associated with different body systems that have similar presentation. Examples:

— Degenerative disc disease and kidney disorders
— Hip muscle strain and prostate cancer
— Inflammatory bowel disease and endometriosis

Integration

--

Diversity Considerations

Struggling students may be reluctant to discuss their answers in class. This activity can be helpful to identify material or topics that require additional study or review.

Eager students might try to dominate the discussion in a way that overwhelms students who have difficulty speaking up. Facilitating the discussion can encourage participation from all students.

Project-Based Activities

Where a Client Might Look

The term "ePatient" refers to consumers that take an active role in their own healthcare. They often seek information from nonclinical resources to answer questions about symptoms and treatments. This is a health literacy activity that helps students recognize where ePatients might look and how to evaluate the information they find.

Ask students to find three different resources that clients might use to answer a health-related question. Have students summarize what they find and rate the quality of the resources. Students can share their findings with the class and compare results.

Materials and Implementation

Computer, tablet, or smartphone and internet connectivity.

Face-to-Face

This could be completed in class as a brief exercise having students work individually or in small groups using a collaborative document.

Online Synchronous

This activity could be adapted to rotate having a few students do this for each module and then present their findings to the class for discussion.

Online Asynchronous

This activity works well as an assignment in an asynchronous class. Students can post their findings to a forum to compare and contrast in the discussion.

Topic Areas

Anatomy & physiology

Pathophysiology

Clinical reasoning

Ethics

PROJECT-BASED ACTIVITIES

Learning Stage Adaptation Examples
Review
Resources aimed at ePatients generally are simplified and use non-clinical language, so this activity can be helpful for students to review new material by comparing what they find to the resources used in class.

Application
As students become confident in finding resources, the class could assemble a list of organizations, databases, and websites they think patients would find for common symptoms, diseases, and disorders.

Integration
--

Diversity Considerations
Advocacy organizations for diseases and disorders are often used by ePatients to gather information on risks, prevention, treatment options, and prognosis. May sites share patient and caregiver stories. This provides a good opportunity for students to learn more about people, communities, and populations affected.

Simple Questions

Using scientific jargon when talking to clients can make students feel important, but it can be confusing for clients. Simplifying information into a client handout can be helpful to use as a guide. Students can also use this exercise as practice for developing marketing materials or social media content.

This activity starts with the instructor listing 3-4 questions that will be used to prepare a single page handout. The students should use an evidence-based approach to preparing the handout. Example: "What is [condition]? Why does [condition] happen? How can massage help? Where can I get more information?"

Each handout should be only one page with references listed on a second page. The students can be creative in the format and layout. Upon completion, students present their handout to the class.

Materials and Implementation

Computer or tablet.

Face-to-Face

This could be completed in class as a brief exercise having students work individually or in small groups using a collaborative document.

Online Synchronous

This activity could be adapted having students post their handouts to a forum or a few students present to the class.

Online Asynchronous

This activity works well as an assignment in an asynchronous class. Students can post their findings to a forum to compare and contrast.

Topic Areas

Pathophysiology

Clinical reasoning

Learning Stage Adaptation Examples

Review

--

Application

Students can reference information from anatomy & physiology and pathophysiology and apply it to common clinical conditions.

Integration

Referencing outcomes research can help students recognize the difference between direct effects of a treatment (e.g. range of motion, pain relief) compared to indirect effects (i.e. psychosocial outcomes like improved mood or stress reduction.)

Diversity Considerations

This activity can emphasize health literacy by adding a requirement for the handouts to be written at a reading level for 6th grade or below.

Physical Assessment Protocol

The ability to perform assessments evolves as students practice and gain experience. As they learn, students can have difficulty trying to figure out when to choose physical assessments and how to perform them effectively and efficiently. This activity has students create their own protocol to follow to help them develop a process and gain confidence.

To begin, have students make a list of every physical assessment they have learned including gait observation, posture analysis, as well as active, passive, and resisted joint range of motion. Have them organize their list to follow a sequence that is logical for them. The result is a customized physical assessment tool.

<u>Materials and Implementation</u>
Computer or tablet.

Face-to-Face

Students can work in small groups during class then complete their assessment as a homework assignment.

Online Synchronous

This could be adapted as a homework assignment.

Online Asynchronous

The class can use a wiki or collaborative document to make a master list of every physical assessment they have learned. After they have completed their own assessment as a homework assignment, they can upload to a forum for review and discussion.

<u>Topic Areas</u>
Kinesiology
Pathophysiology
Clinical reasoning

Learning Stage Adaptation Examples

Review

The initial part of this activity—making a master list of all physical assessments—is a good opportunity for students to reflect what they have learned. This could be incorporated at the end of different course units or modules.

Application

This activity requires students to construct an organized approach to physical assessments. Have students share their assessments in small groups to compare different approaches and get feedback.

Integration

Students can test out their assessment tool during clinical practice and revise as they learn. The final result can be incorporated as part of their portfolio.

Diversity Considerations

This activity requires students to apply concepts and organize their own process in a way that makes sense to them individually. Faculty and other students may follow a different approach; this should be taken into account when students share their assessment tools with others for feedback and/or try to practice the tool they created.

HANDS OFF!

Psychosocial Assessment Tool

Psychosocial outcomes are often used in research to assess effects of treatment. The Profile of Mood States, Functional Assessment of Chronic Illness Therapy, and other assessments used in research provide insight into quality of life, mood, and emotions. These may not be targeted as intentional outcomes of a session, but assessing a client's perceptions and experience can provide insight into the value a client places on treatment.

This activity asks students to create a short survey to assess psychosocial measures. First, the students identify different variables they think are relevant or important. Then they can construct a tool using a numerical ranking or Likert scale. After a draft is completed, the students can present it to the class for feedback.

Materials and Implementation

Computer or tablet.

Sample psychosocial surveys and/or research articles.

Face-to-Face

Students can work in small groups using a collaborative document.

Online Synchronous

Students can work in breakout rooms and use a collaborative document to construct their survey.

Online Asynchronous

Students could work asynchronously in a collaborative document that can be posted to a discussion forum for feedback from the class.

Topic Areas

Pathophysiology

Clinical reasoning

Learning Stage Adaptation Examples

Review

This activity can work well to help students review after a course unit or module on the brain and behavior.

Application

Once the assessments are completed, students could apply different assessments to case studies and compare reliability of the results.

Integration

This activity could ask the students to pair their assessments with examples of physical measurements to recognize the relationship among quality of life domains.

Diversity Considerations

The concept of quality of life can vary among different ethnic and cultural groups. Socioeconomic status also factors into quality of life. Encourage students to think broadly about the surrounding community to identify variables for this assessment.

Study Skills

Create a Study Guide

Teaching students how to effectively use course materials can help them become more effective learners at any age. Instead of giving students a study guide, have them make their own. Organizing notes from textbooks, lectures, and assignments into a study guide can help students review and recognize how multiple resources contribute to learning. For this activity, students work in small groups to create a study guide. This can be to prepare for an exam, or the students can collaborate on ongoing development of a study guide throughout the course.

Materials and Implementation

Paper and pen/pencil or computer/tablet

Class notes, textbooks, workbooks, and assignments

Face-to-Face

Students can work in small groups using a collaborative document.

Online Synchronous

Students can work in breakout rooms and use a collaborative document to construct their study guide.

Online Asynchronous

Students could work asynchronously in a collaborative document. A deadline for completion would be necessary.

Topic Areas

Anatomy & physiology

Kinesiology

Pathophysiology

Clinical reasoning

Ethics

Learning Stage Adaptation Examples

Review

Students condense material from a course module or unit into a glossary or table. The focus is on terms and definitions to help students recognize concepts and relate them to each other.

Application

Students make concept maps to place terms/concepts and connect them using color-coding or drawings to show how they relate to each other.

Integration

When this activity has been used in a foundational or didactic class, students can take that study guide and add to it for courses that require clinical reasoning.

This activity can also be used for an ethics course to help students reference concepts to case scenarios.

Diversity Considerations

Students have different levels of academic preparedness. Novice students, slower learners, and students from disadvantaged backgrounds can struggle to keep up in courses. Forming groups with a mix of different types of students can encourage peer learning and make this a valuable activity.

HANDS OFF!

Not Quite Open Book

This activity helps students learn to develop and use a memory aid. When resources are allowed to be used during tests, the process of preparing the resource helps students study. Students work during class in small groups to create their own information resource for an upcoming test. The resource could be written on a single sheet of paper, an index card, or even a plain t-shirt (for the students to wear during the test.)

The class can start with a review led by the instructor. The students identify topics that they need help remembering, or information that requires memorization. Then. they design their resource. The students can take the resource home, edit, add material, and practice using it. Prior to the test, the instructor reviews the resources to ensure that they meet criteria set forth in class and academic integrity guidelines.

Materials and Implementation

Blank paper, index cards, or plain white t-shirts, and pens.

Face-to-Face

During a review session, students can make lists of information they want to include and then prepare their individual resources.

Online Synchronous

--

Online Asynchronous

--

Topic Areas

Anatomy & physiology

Pathophysiology

Learning Stage Adaptation Examples

Review

Preparation of the resource requires that students review course material.

Application

Because students have a resource during the exam, critical thinking activities can be incorporated in exam questions to help students apply concepts.

Integration

Students may be able to more easily learn to synthesize information when they are able to reference a resource that they worked to create.

Diversity Considerations

For students that lack academic preparedness, this is a good opportunity for a semi-directed study activity. When students work in small groups, pairing high achievers with struggling students can provide a peer-learning opportunity. To hold all students accountable to participate, include a self-assessment asking each student to describe their role and indicate the percent of effort they contributed to the overall group effort.

Wiki Me This

Encouraging students to engage with each other and provide support can be valuable. It may help high achievers develop leadership skills and can provide support to struggling students. This activity is a class collaboration on a shared reference resource in a collaborative document or using the wiki feature in a course management system. The instructor can introduce the activity by posting major topics and important concepts then encouraging students to add their own information. This can grow into an encyclopedia for course material. As students add more material, it becomes a place where students can clarify information for each other. The instructor can review the wiki to identify information that needs to be reviewed in class.

Materials and Implementation

Laptop or tablet and Wi-Fi.

Face-to-Face

This activity could be introduced in class for students to brainstorm information they think should be included.

Online Synchronous

Like the face-to-face setting, the activity can be introduced during a class meeting. Students can be assigned homework to make additions to the wiki.

Online Asynchronous

This activity works best in an asynchronous format because it provides an alternative place for students to communicate with each other.

Topic Areas

Anatomy & physiology

Pathophysiology

Ethics

Learning Stage Adaptation Examples

Review

This is an excellent opportunity for students to review course material and identify important concepts. If used in didactic or foundational courses, students could be encouraged to save a copy of the final resource for use in more advanced courses.

Application

Students can provide more substantial information by defining and making associations between different concepts.

Integration

Students can provide more thorough summaries of information, including analysis or examples along with references.

Diversity Considerations

High achieving students may be more eager to participate than struggling students. When this is the case, encouraging all students to add material or edit to their own level of comfort or ability can meet students on their level. Alternatively, this activity could require a specific number of contributions from each student. This could encourage students who may be reluctant to otherwise participate in the activity.

HANDS OFF!

Short Videos

This is a peer-tutoring activity that uses a creative approach with students creating and sharing short video tutorials (1-2 minutes long.) These could be animations, mini slide presentations, poetry, or music that explains a course concept. Students can be assigned a topic from a list—to ensure that all topics are adequately covered, and then make the videos as a homework assignment. Then, the videos can be shown during class and followed by a discussion. The creative aspect of this activity can be fun while the results provide a way for the instructor to gauge how well students are retaining and applying course material.

Materials and Implementation

Cellphone camera, webcam, presentation or animation software. Computer and projector to play in class.

Face-to-Face

This activity works well as an introduction to a class session or a reflection at the end of class. For large classes, the videos can be archived for students to review.

Online Synchronous

Students could view the videos as an assignment before class and then bring feedback to the online meeting for discussion.

Online Asynchronous

Students could view the videos as an assignment and then participate in a discussion forum.

Topic Areas

Anatomy & physiology

Pathophysiology

Clinical reasoning

Ethics

Learning Stage Adaptation Examples

Review

This is a good review activity for introductory material. The instructor can compile a list of topics or concepts that are complex or challenging for students. This can be used to create a "library" of videos that can be retained as a study resource for the remainder of the course. Examples:

— Demonstrate how to perform range of motion tests.
— Trace origins & insertions of muscles and demonstrate actions.

Application

The assignment can take a problem-solving approach by having students answer a complex question. Examples:

— Demonstrate a practice interview for a client with chronic idiopathic pain.
— Describe the difference between an employee and independent contractor.

Integration

This activity can require students to reframe a topic or add additional layers of information. Examples:

— Summarize considerations for a client with type 2 diabetes that is well-controlled.
— Role-play a client scenario (e.g. request work outside scope of practice, examples of dual relationships, transference.)

Diversity Considerations

For students who are creative by nature, this type of activity can be highly engaging. However, students who are not particularly creative may struggle to approach the assignment. They may also have difficulty seeing the relevance of this activity. Encouraging all students to embrace different instructional approaches can help them recognize value in creative activities.

Infographic

Infographics are visual representations of data, complex concepts, or processes. Preparation of the infographic requires background research into the topic, organization of ideas, and planning the project. This activity can be done individually, in pairs, or small groups. Begin by providing several samples of infographics to help students become familiar with the concept. Then, identify a target audience for the project, suggest resource material, and assign (or have students choose) topics. Allow time with this activity for providing informal feedback to the students.

<u>Materials and Implementation</u>
Laptop or tablet with an app that can integrate drawing and text.

Face-to-Face

This can be started as an in-class activity with a brainstorming and planning session. Then it can continue as an assignment with the finished product presented in class.

Online Synchronous

This can be started as an in-class activity using breakout rooms for a brainstorming and planning session. Then it can continue as an assignment, with the finished product posted to a forum for the class to review.

Online Asynchronous

This is effective as a self-paced assignment. The final product can be posted to a forum for the class to review.

<u>Topic Areas</u>
Kinesiology
Pathophysiology
Clinical reasoning
Ethics

Learning Stage Adaptation Examples

Review

This provides a good review for complex material that requires students to link ideas together. This could be done with the entire class working on the same topic, or dividing topics among the class. Examples:
— Biomechanical differences between walking and running
— The process of informed consent
— Effects of a cerebrovascular accident on the body

Application

The students can explore interrelated health and well-being concepts to recognize indirect effects of treatment.
— Explore factors that could be used to assess effects of treatment on quality of life.
— Summarize multiple dimensions of well-being and how they could be impacted by treatment

Integration

This is a nice activity to challenge thinking about evidence-based practice because it requires students to weigh theory with outcomes research.
— Identify assessments for treatment of a client who is in remission from prostate cancer.
— Differentiate between potential contraindications and precautions in treatment design for a client with hypertension.

Diversity Considerations

For students who are creative by nature, this type of activity can be highly engaging. However, students who are not particularly creative may struggle to approach the assignment. Having students work in small groups can help to balance different perceptions and help students to get the most from this activity.

HANDS OFF!

Fix My Class Notes

Learning to take notes is an art. Students who struggle with notes may be hampered by identifying relevant information, organizing material, and effectively utilizing notes to study. In this activity, students work in pairs or small groups to review each other's class notes and make suggestions for improvement.

Start by having all students open their book, workbook, or notebooks to the same topic. Then ask them to pass their notes to their partner or another person in their group. Have them compare and contrast the presentation and contents of their notes, and make suggestions for additions, deletions, or reorganization. They can use highlighter or sticky notes to "flag" important concepts.

Materials and Implementation

Notebooks containing class notes.

Pens, pencils, sticky notes, or highlighters.

Face-to-Face

This activity works well to start an in-class review at the end of a course unit or module. After the working session, students can share new ideas or information with the class.

Online Synchronous

--

Online Asynchronous

Students can collaborate through a discussion forum to compare and contrast scanned PDFs of written or typed notes.

Topic Areas

Anatomy & physiology

Kinesiology

Pathophysiology

Ethics

Learning Stage Adaptation Examples

Review

This is an excellent activity to include early in a term when students are still working on study skills. It can also be effective later in the term after students have completed enough assessments that help them recognize when they might need to find new ways to study.

Application

This can help students who are struggling with problem solving or relating ideas to each other. Color-coding the notes with sticky notes or highlighters can help identify solutions.

Integration

Students can explain a topic to their partner or group and then review similarities or differences in how the topic is notated.

Diversity Considerations

Students who struggle with notes may feel overwhelmed, but peer learning can be useful in this context. Care should be taken to make sure that all students are supportive of each other by taking a solutions approach to improve/enhance notes.

Some students may be protective of their notes if notebooks are expensive for them. Other students may be reluctant to share resources. Having another student write in their notebook may feel invasive. To alleviate anxiousness, allow other students to write in pencil or on a separate sheet of paper.

HANDS OFF!

Mind Your MCQs

Successful test taking requires a combination of knowledge and skills. Practice tests are only one way to help students gain skills and confidence. Learning to write multiple choice questions (MCQs) helps to teach students about question design and format. It can help them learn to recognize important information in the stem, identify distractors, and develop strategies to evaluate answer choices.

For this activity, students work in small groups to write a short set of multiple-choice questions for a course unit or module. They choose the question topics, write the stem/problem, and then list possible answers. Once each group completes a short "test," the groups take turns testing the rest of the class.

Materials and Implementation

Laptop or tablet. Blank paper to record answers.

Face-to-Face

This can be a fun activity that promotes discussion when the question writers are asked to provide rationale for their selection of topics and answer options.

Online Synchronous

Students could work in breakout rooms and then all questions could be compiled for the students to use for a practice test.

Online Asynchronous

Students can prepare a practice test to share with the class for review and discussion in a forum.

Topic Areas

Anatomy & physiology

Pathophysiology

Ethics

Learning Stage Adaptation Examples

Review

This is an excellent activity to include on an ongoing basis at the end of course units or modules. Students can prepare 5-question "tests" for each unit to assess important information. As the students make progress through a course, they would be creating their own practice test bank.

Application

To add a layer of complexity to this activity, have one student write the stem/problem and then another student prepares the list of response items.

Integration

Encourage the students to progress beyond memory-based questions to require higher level thinking. Example:

— Contraction of the rotator cuff muscles produces which movements? (memory based question)
— The activity of the shoulder joint that occurs when a person reaches up to pull a t-shirt on over their head requires which type of movement involving the rotator cuff muscles (memory plus application question)

Diversity Considerations

Students who have been tutored in test-taking skills may excel at this activity. However, students who lack adequate academic preparedness may struggle. This is a good opportunity to take a thoughtful approach to forming small groups so students can learn from their peers.

Peer Teaching

Fuzzy or Clear

Sometimes students have difficulty admitting when they are struggling to master course material. This activity provides an informal assessment through gamification, review, and peer-learning. Each student prepares a two-sided sheet of paper. On one side they write the word "Fuzzy" on the other the word "Clear." This should be in large letters so that the words can be seen by the entire class.

The instructor starts the activity by presenting a term or concept to the class. It can be read aloud, shown on a slide, or written on a white board. Students are given a few seconds to think about how well they understand the term or concept. Then they hold up the sign to indicate whether they think they have a "clear" understanding or if they are "fuzzy" about the topic. The instructor then calls on a student who is holding the "clear" sign to explain their understanding of the term or concept to the class.

Materials and Implementation
Blank paper, pen/pencil.

Face-to-Face

This is a fun activity for in-person classes. If possible, configure the seating arrangement so students can see each other.

Online Synchronous

This can be adapted by using webcams and the gallery view so all students are visible. Students can hold their sign in front of the webcam.

Online Asynchronous

\--

Topic Areas
Anatomy & physiology
Kinesiology
Pathophysiology
Ethics

Learning Stage Adaptation Examples

Review

This activity can be a good review towards the end of a course unit or module, or prior to an exam. Allow adequate time for the instructor to give feedback between terms or concepts. This may be necessary to supplement or correct what the "clear" student explains.

Application

This activity can provide an excellent opportunity for the instructor to assess how well the students can break down complex concepts or interpret information. Asking a "clear" student to identify resources that helped them understand the term or concept can be helpful to other students—and the instructor.

Integration

When complex information is used in this activity, encouraging the students to compare, contrast, and provide examples can help layer ideas for the students to take away.

Diversity Considerations

The combination of gamification and an informal assessment can help draw out struggling students who may not be willing to seek help.

Hearing a peer explain a term or concept can be useful to collaboratively work through difficult aspects. This interdependency can benefit the "clear" and "fuzzy" student.

If there is a group of students who are consistently "clear" rotating among them can be helpful so that different students get a chance to contribute.

I Could Teach That

Students can gain a deeper understanding of material when they practice teaching something. For this activity, students are asked to identify one topic or concept that they know very well—so well that they could teach it. All topics are compiled on a whiteboard or flipchart. Then students can break out into small groups and teach their selected topic/concept to others. To help manage time, small groups can have 3-4 students with each student allotted 5 minutes to teach. At the conclusion of the peer teaching, the whole class can be invited to reflect on what they believe they did well—and what they learned.

Materials and Implementation

Whiteboard or flipchart.

Face-to-Face

This activity can easily be incorporated into a face-to-face class session. It can serve as a review or an icebreaker.

Online Synchronous

This activity can be done using breakout rooms for the small groups.

Online Asynchronous

Students could write short summaries that they share in a discussion forum with a small group. This would permit the opportunity for group members to ask questions and seek clarifications. Then, all of the material can be shared with the class.

Topic Areas

Anatomy & physiology

Kinesiology

Pathophysiology

Clinical reasoning

Learning Stage Adaptation Examples

Review

Using this activity to help students review material can build confidence when they are able to identify something that they know well. Example: in kinesiology, ask students to teach joint actions or synergist muscles.

Application

This can be a nice activity at the beginning of an advanced class by asking students to review material from a foundational course. Example: for a pathophysiology unit on circulatory disorders, narrow the topics/concepts to have students select from the cardiovascular, lymphatic, and respiratory systems.

Integration

Asking students to select topics that require connections between didactic course material and clinical or applied courses can help them recognize threads in the curriculum. Example: in an ethics course, ask students to identify scenarios that would require extra considerations in treatment design.

Diversity Considerations

Some students may be reluctant to speak up in class. Having them work in small groups can build confidence and develop presentation skills.

Care should be taken to monitor groups so that all students are given an opportunity to participate as teachers.

HANDS OFF!

A Little Help Here

Students may feel lonely if they struggle with course material. Sometimes it can be difficult to identify where they get stuck and figure out how to get help. This activity works through that by operating on the assumption that all students need help with something. Students are asked to identify a topic or concept that needs clarification or more explanation. Each student writes the topic on an index card and the cards are handed into the instructor. After shuffling the cards, each student is given a randomly-selected card. They read the new card and identify where they would go to get more information to help them better understand the topic or concept.

Materials and Implementation
Blank index cards, pen/pencil.

Face-to-Face

This activity can be done within small groups. The students write their suggestions on the back of the cards which can be left on a table for students to take as they exit the classroom.

Online Synchronous

This activity can be done using a wiki or collaborative document to identify topics/concepts. Students can work in breakout rooms to discuss and write their suggestions in the collaborative document.

Online Asynchronous

--

Topic Areas
Anatomy & physiology
Kinesiology
Pathophysiology
Clinical reasoning

Learning Stage Adaptation Examples
Review
This can be a useful activity for the end of a course unit or module to help students identify resources to help study for an exam.
Application
This activity could be helpful at the introduction of an advanced course that requires students to draw upon foundational material. To help students make connections, the instructor could provide a list of topics/concepts that are prerequisite for the upper level course. Students would be asked to choose from the list.
Integration
Students could be asked to make a diagram of multiple information sources and grade the quality of the information provided. For example, drawing a staircase that places a consumer website at the bottom, then lists trade magazines, textbooks, class notes, peer-reviewed journals in order of importance.

Diversity Considerations

The key takeaway from this activity is the focus on identifying resources that can be used for help, not explaining the topic or concept. The topics/concepts identified by the students are anonymously submitted. This helps to add a layer of comfort—no one knows who is associated with a particular topic or concept.

This activity can provide the instructor with an informal assessment to identify material in need of review. It can also be helpful for the instructor to build a reservoir of additional resources that the students recommend—or use—to supplement course material.

What Did I Say? 1

For challenging concepts, peer-to-peer teaching is often very useful. This activity uses paraphrasing to have students teach each other. Working in pairs, the activity begins with one student designated the "Explainer" and their partner the "Learner." The Explainer summarizes a concept and then the Learner paraphrases what they understand from what they heard. It is important that the Learner not repeat verbatim, but paraphrases. The Explainer listens carefully to identify similarities and differences in the Learner's interpretation of the original explanation. If there are notable differences, the Explainer tries again—using different words—and the Learner paraphrases what they understand. Once they are in agreement, the students switch roles.

Materials and Implementation

This activity should be timed to match complexity of the material covered in the course unit or module.

Students should have course notes, textbooks, and other resources to use as references.

Face-to-Face

This activity works well in a face-to-face class when the room can be reconfigured to provide space for students to work in pairs.

Online Synchronous

This could be modified to have pairs of students demonstrate the activity for the class to observe.

Online Asynchronous

--

Topic Areas
Anatomy & physiology
Pathophysiology
Clinical reasoning
Ethics

Learning Stage Adaptation Examples

Review

This can be a useful activity for the end of a course unit or module to help students work through complicated concepts. Examples:
— The difference between exocrine and endocrine glands
— Structure and function of different layers of skin

Application

This is an excellent activity to help students compare and contrast related concepts. Examples:
— Why outcomes from transient ischemic attack differ from a cerebrovascular accident
— The relationship between risk factors for type 2 diabetes and heart disease

Integration

When students struggle with critical thinking, this type of activity can help them identify key concepts and break them down. Examples:
— What different range of motion tests for the shoulder joint and shoulder girdle would reveal
— How a multidimensional assessment could help design a treatment plan

Diversity Considerations

This type of activity may be challenging for slower learners, English-language learners, or students who are reluctant to speak up in class. Encouraging students to use reference material and collaborate can help them work together as a group.

This activity also encourages students to be respectful and listen carefully.

HANDS OFF!

What Did I Say? 2

This activity uses paraphrasing to stimulate discussion and analysis of a topic in peer teaching. Students separate into small groups. Each group designates an "Explainer" and "Respondent." The class is presented with a concept or problem. The Explainer summarizes an answer for the small group. The Respondent paraphrases the summary without correcting the answer. Each small group then discusses the summary and clarifies information until they agree on their answer. The class comes together, and each Respondent presents the group's answer. The class can review differences in the answers. The activity can be repeated for new questions.

Materials and Implementation
A prepared list of concepts or problems for the students to review.

Face-to-Face

This activity works well in a face-to-face class with students sitting in small groups.

Online Synchronous

The small groups could use breakout rooms to review several questions. The groups can rotate the roles of Explainer and Respondent. When the class comes back together their responses can either be presented orally or added to a discussion forum for students and instructor to review.

Online Asynchronous

--

Topic Areas
Anatomy & physiology
Pathophysiology
Clinical reasoning
Ethics

Learning Stage Adaptation Examples

Review

This can be a useful activity for the end of a course unit or module to help students work through complicated concepts. Examples:
- Complications from congestive heart failure
- Symptoms of traumatic brain injury

Application

This is an excellent activity to help students compare and contrast related concepts. Examples:
- Hyponatremia and dehydration
- Alzheimer Disease and dementia
- Temporomandibular joint dysfunction and migraine

Integration

When students struggle with critical thinking, this type of activity can help them identify key concepts and break them down. Examples:
- Dietary, behavioral, and iatrogenic risk factors for muscle cramps
- The pathophysiology of whiplash

Diversity Considerations

Some students may be reluctant to speak up in class. This activity provides them with an opportunity to make a contribution in a smaller group which may help them be more comfortable.

This activity also encourages students to be respectful and listen carefully.

Explain that to Grandma

The way a professional explains something to a colleague is different from the way they need to explain to a client. Students sometimes use jargon in order to appear intelligent, but this can make it difficult to talk with clients. Breaking down complex clinical information into easily understandable, scientifically accurate language takes practice. This activity uses a combination of peer teaching and role-play to give students a thorough exploration of a concept that they would need to learn how to explain to a client.

Working in pairs, one student explains the same concept twice to their partner. The first time is as if their partner is a colleague. The second time is as if it is to a friend, relative, or client by breaking it down into easy-to-understand language. The explanation must be accurate, but no jargon is allowed. Then, each pair of students summarizes key differences in the approach and then switch roles to explain a different concept.

Materials and Implementation

A prepared list of concepts or problems for the students to review.

Face-to-Face

This activity works well in a face-to-face class when the room can be reconfigured to provide space for students to work in pairs.

Online Synchronous

This could be modified to have pairs of students demonstrate the activity for the class to observe.

Online Asynchronous

Students could make short videos of themselves explaining a concept for a partner to review and give feedback.

Topic Areas
Pathophysiology
Clinical reasoning

Learning Stage Adaptation Examples
Review

This can be a useful activity for the end of a course unit or module or in preparatory sessions for practicum. Examples:
- Why different types of assessments can help provide insight into factors that contribute to chronic back pain
- The impact of aging on bone density

Application

This is an excellent activity to help students compare and contrast related concepts. Examples:
- Atherosclerosis and arteriosclerosis
- Physical and psycho-emotional effects of disordered eating

Integration

Students can work through this activity to parse information about complex or chronic health problems. Examples:
- Depression as a comorbidity in multiple sclerosis, cancer, or rheumatoid arthritis
- Dementia that develops in individuals with Parkinson's disease

Diversity Considerations

Recognizing different ways to explain the same information can help students improve communication skills. This is especially important for students who rely on jargon to try to impress others. Students can practice finding their professional voice through different types of conversations.

Games

HANDS OFF!

Name that Term

This activity is based off of the music trivia game show *Name That Tune* where people compete to name a tune in the fewest notes possible. For this activity teams of students test their knowledge of terms by competing with each other to by trying to identify a term in the fewest clues possible.

The class is separated into teams. The instructor states the general category for the first term. Each team confers to decide how many clues they need to identify the term. The team that states the fewest clues is given that number of clues by the instructor. If they are successful in naming the term, they win a point. If they are not successful, the other team gets a chance to name the term. The team with the most points at the end of the game is declared the winner.

<u>Materials and Implementation</u>

A prepared list of terms and at least 4 or 5 clues for each term.

Face-to-Face

This activity works well in a face-to-face class when the room can be reconfigured to provide space for teams of students to sit on opposite sides of the room.

Online Synchronous

This activity could be modified to have two teams, and one representative from each team competing at a time.

Online Asynchronous

--

<u>Topic Areas</u>
Anatomy & physiology
Kinesiology
Pathophysiology
Ethics

GAMES

Learning Stage Adaptation Examples

Review

This activity works nicely as a low-stakes review when students need to be able to recall information. Example:
— The terms could be muscles and the clues would be origins, insertions, actions, innervation, and/or blood supply for the muscles.

Application

To help students compare and contrast different disorders. The clues could be anatomical structures, risk factors, or symptoms. Examples:
— Heart valve disorders, coronary artery disease, atherosclerosis, arteriosclerosis
— Parkinson's disease, Huntington disease, Alzheimer disease, Lewy body dementia, traumatic brain injury

Integration

--

Diversity Considerations

Students who are reluctant to speak up in class may feel challenged if they are in a group with outspoken students. Teams should be encouraged to collaborate so that all voices are heard, and everyone has a chance to participate.

This may be a challenging activity for English-language learners if they struggle with terms and definitions. If that is the case, after each point the instructor can reveal the term and definition from the glossary used in the course. This can reinforce the information provided in the clues and give all students the opportunity to review.

HANDS OFF!

Zebra or Horse?

The saying "when you hear hoof beats, think horse, not zebra" is a reminder that there are similarities—and differences—between rare and common diseases and disorders. This game presents the opportunity to differentiate the more common diseases and disorders (horses) from rare conditions (zebras.)

The instructor prepares the list of topics for the activity. It can be the names of diseases, disorders, signs, or symptoms from the course unit or module. The class is separated into several teams. Each team prepares two sheets of paper: one with "Zebra" and the other with "Horse." The instructor reads the topic and teams are given a moment to confer. Then they indicate whether it is rare (by holding up the zebra sign) or common (holding up the horse sign.) The instructor can ask teams to defend their answer.

Materials and Implementation
Blank paper, pen/pencil
A prepared list of diseases or disorders to review.

Face-to-Face

This activity works well in a face-to-face class when the room can be reconfigured to provide space for teams of students to sit on opposite sides of the room.

Online Synchronous

This can be adapted to be an individual activity with students using webcams and the gallery view so all students are visible. Students can hold their sign in front of the webcam.

Online Asynchronous

--

Topic Areas
Pathophysiology
Clinical reasoning

Learning Stage Adaptation Examples

Review

This activity can be a good review allowing adequate time for teams to defend their answers. An example of symptoms or conditions that could promote healthy debate:

— Chest pain, unexplained muscle weakness, blurred vision
— Type 1 diabetes, fascioscapular humeral muscular dystrophy, migraine, conjunctivitis

Application

This activity can provide an excellent opportunity for the instructor to help students identify important information about conditions.

— Persistent back pain, dyspnea, unilateral foot edema
— Hypertension, hypotension, hyperlipidemia, familial hypercholesterolemia

Integration

--

Diversity Considerations

Student knowledge about diseases and disorders is not only what is learned in class, but also is informed by their family and community. A condition that may seem rare to one student may be perceived as common to another student (e.g. Tay-Sachs disease or Sickle cell disease.) The instructor should keep this possibility in mind when selecting diseases or disorders for this activity.

HANDS OFF!

Mnemonics

Memorization is not easy for every student. A mnemonic device is a learning technique that can help students organize, retain, and retrieve information by using a pattern. Students can be challenged to come up with a creative and unique mnemonic or acrostic. A Mnemonic is a string of letters to help remember words or a sequence. Examples:

Airway Breathing Circulation (ABCs) to remember the order for helping a patient in cardiopulmonary resuscitation

Supraspinatus, Infraspinatus, Teres minor, Subscapularis (SITS) to remember the muscles of the rotator cuff.

Mnemonics can be done with several teams covering different topics from a course or unit. Each team collaborates to develop a mnemonic, and the results are shared with the class.

Materials and Implementation

Face-to-Face

This activity can take time to complete, it could be started with a team discussion in class and then continue as an assignment to be submitted later to allow students to refine their work.

Online Synchronous

This activity could start by using breakout rooms and a collaborative document during class. Then it can continue as an assignment to be submitted later to allow students to refine.

Online Asynchronous

This works well with students working in a collaborative document.

Topic Areas

Anatomy & physiology

Pathophysiology

Clinical reasoning

Learning Stage Adaptation Examples

Review

This is a good activity to prepare students to retain and retrieve information for an exam. There are many examples of medical mnemonics. Some popular topics include:
- The cranial nerves
- A protocol to assess pain
- Position of the carpal bones
- Rotator cuff muscles
- Cushing syndrome presentation
- Osteoporosis treatment
- Hypertension risk factors

Application

--

Integration

--

Diversity Considerations

For students that can easily memorize information, it may be difficult to involve them in this type of activity. It may take effort to encourage them to collaborate with their team.

Students that have difficulty with memorization can benefit from learning how to identify patterns.

HANDS OFF!

Tennis 1

This activity is based on a repetition exercise from the Meisner acting technique that is used to teach actors to listen and pay attention to each other. This version helps students become familiar with vocabulary and terms that are related to each other. Pairs of students stand facing each other and toss terms back and forth. One partner opens the activity by saying a term. Their partner repeats the term and they keep repeating the term until one of them thinks of a related term. That partner says the new term, and then they must repeat it until one of them thinks of another related term.

This activity can be timed for 1-2 minutes for each pair of students. Time permitting, they can switch partners and repeat the game. It works well for a warm-up activity at the beginning of a class session, or a wrap-up activity at the end of class.

Materials and Implementation

Face-to-Face

This activity works well in a face-to-face class where there is space for pairs of students to stand facing each other. To keep the activity flowing, students can toss an object to their partner as they say their word.

Online Synchronous

This can be adapted to have one pair of students participate at a time.

Online Asynchronous

--

Topic Areas
Anatomy & physiology
Pathophysiology
Ethics

GAMES

Learning Stage Adaptation Examples

Review

This is an excellent vocabulary-building activity for a course unit or module. Beginning students can have a glossary on hand to refer to before they start to play.

Application

To help students work through more advanced concepts, the instructor could prepare index cards with opening terms.

Integration

--

Diversity Considerations

This activity can help students become comfortable saying medical and scientific terminology. It may initially be challenging for English-language learners. Encouraging students to be patient with their partners can foster empathy and help all students improve verbal skills.

HANDS OFF!

Tennis 2

This is a more advanced variation on *Tennis 1* that requires students to relate terms instead of repeating them. Working in pairs, have students stand and face each other. One student tosses out a term, and their partner responds with a related term. Then they go back and forth each adding a related term until they run out of terms. When a student cannot think of a related term, their partner is declared the winner.

To challenge the class, this can be played as a knockout game. Winners from each round can be paired up to play against each other for subsequent rounds. The winner from the final pair can be declared vocabulary champion for the day.

Materials and Implementation

Face-to-Face

This activity works well in a face-to-face class where there is space for pairs of students to stand facing each other. To keep the activity flowing, students can toss an object to their partner as they say their word.

Online Synchronous

This can be adapted two have one pair of students participate at a time.

Online Asynchronous

--

Topic Areas
Anatomy & physiology
Pathophysiology
Ethics

Learning Stage Adaptation Examples

Review

This is an excellent vocabulary-building activity for a course unit or module. Beginning students can have a glossary on hand to refer to before they start to play.

Application

To help students work through more advanced concepts, the instructor could prepare index cards with opening terms.

Integration

--

Diversity Considerations

This activity can help students become comfortable saying medical and scientific terminology. It may initially be challenging for English-language learners. Encouraging students to be patient with their partners can foster empathy and help all students improve verbal skills.

HANDS OFF!

Hangman

This is a low-tech way to review vocabulary and spelling. Using blank paper, a whiteboard, or a flipchart, a student draws out a series of blanks that correspond to the number of letters in a vocabulary word. The other students take turns guessing letters. When the guess is correct, the letter is inserted into the word. When a guess is wrong, portions of a stick figure are drawn to tally the number of wrong guesses. The goal is to guess the word before the entire stick figure is completed. If the stick figure is completed before the word is guessed, the person drawing gets a point. If a student guesses the word correctly, they win a point.

Small groups of students can play several rounds of this game taking turns testing each other on vocabulary. At the end of the games, the student with the most points wins.

Materials and Implementation

Blank paper, whiteboard, or a flipchart; pen, pencil, or markers.

Face-to-Face

This activity works nicely in class with space to configure students in small groups.

Online Synchronous

This can be played using breakout rooms and a drawing software program.

Online Asynchronous

--

Topic Areas

Anatomy & physiology

Kinesiology

Pathophysiology

Clinical reasoning

Ethics

Learning Stage Adaptation Examples

Review

This is an excellent vocabulary building exercise. For course units or modules with very long words, the gallows could be drawn to extend the number of options to guess. After the game, the class can discuss what words were easiest or more challenging to figure out.

Application

--

Integration

--

Diversity Considerations

This game can be controversial because it is perceived by some as offensive. A variation is to tally the wrong answers by using hash marks or drawing something different (e.g. tree, house, cat, or horse, or just a stick figure wearing a hat.) A key to the variation is to make sure that there is a way for the students who are guessing to know how many guesses they have remaining to try to figure out the word.

HANDS OFF!

Match Game

This low-tech review matches terms or concepts to help students review vocabulary. Using index cards that are all the same color, write terms or concepts on pairs of cards. Lay the cards face down on a large table. This can work with 9 terms or concepts (18 cards total, 6 per row) or 15 terms or concepts (30 cards total, 10 per row.)

Have students take turns flipping over cards—two at a time—to look for a match. If the cards do not match, the students turn those cards face down in the same position. When a match is revealed, that pair of cards is left facing up or removed from the game. Students take turns and keep playing until all matching pairs are found.

For an added challenge, have students create the games. They can work in small groups to create games for other groups to play.

Materials and Implementation

Face-to-Face

This works well for small classes or small groups of students in larger classes.

Online Synchronous

One or more match games could be made using an app.

Online Asynchronous

--

Topic Areas
Anatomy & physiology
Kinesiology
Pathophysiology
Ethics

GAMES

Learning Stage Adaptation Examples

Review

This is an excellent vocabulary building activity for a course unit or module. Students can practice saying them when they find a match.

Application

To help students apply concepts, the pairs of cards can have related concepts. Examples:

— Cerebellum – coordination
— Temporal lobe – hearing
— Hypothalamus – temperature
— Frontal lobe – speech
— Occipital lobe – vision

Integration

--

Diversity Considerations

For slower learners or English-language learners, this activity can work very well in small groups by providing a low-stakes environment to help with familiarity of terms. Referring to a glossary after conclusion of the game could be helpful for supplemental review.

HANDS OFF!

In a Flash

Students pair up and create a deck of 20 flashcards with terms or concepts they think are most important for the class. One side of the card has the term or name of the concept, the other side has a definition/explanation. After each pair of students makes their deck of flashcards, the deck is passed to a different pair of students to use for a speed review.

One student ("Giver") tests the other ("Receiver") by showing a card. If the Receiver needs help, the Giver can provide clues. The Receiver needs to try to answer all cards in the deck. Wrong answers (or cards the Receiver passes on) are put into a separate pile so the Giver can return back to those and let the Receiver try again. Pairs of students then can swap cards with another pair and play again by switching Giver and Receiver roles.

Materials and Implementation

Blank index cards, pens/pencils.

In lieu of making flash cards a pre-published deck could be used and split up into smaller decks for the class.

Face-to-Face

This activity works nicely in class with space to configure students in pairs.

Online Synchronous

--

Online Asynchronous

Students can use an app to create a deck of flashcards to share with a partner for review.

Topic Areas

Anatomy & physiology

Pathophysiology

Learning Stage Adaptation Examples

Review

The process of making flashcards provides a review for the students. This is an excellent vocabulary building exercise. It is also helpful for any information that students will need to rapidly recall.

Application

Students get practice explaining concepts and paraphrasing definitions as they build their flashcard deck and when they play the game.

Integration

The activity can be enhanced by asking students to reference foundational information either when preparing the flashcard deck or when they answer as the Receiver.

Diversity Considerations

This activity can engage students who are reluctant to speak up in class. For underprepared students who struggle with study skills, this activity can demonstrate a low cost/low-tech way they can create a study resource and use it to review course material. Encouraging high achieving students to partner with struggling students presents an opportunity for peer tutoring.

HANDS OFF!

Got Your Back

This activity is based on a party game that is used to help guests get to know each other. The instructor prepares name tags with terms. There should be enough terms for each student in the class. When students arrive at class, without seeing the information a nametag is placed on each of them: on the back right between the shoulder blades.

The students then walk around to each other and "yes" or "no" questions to try and figure out their term. Once they think they have the answer, they report it to the instructor. When the student has the right term, the instructor peels off the tag and offers it to the student to place on their chest like a typical nametag.

This activity is a good icebreaker.

Materials and Implementation

Prepared adhesive name tags

Face-to-Face

This activity is designed for a face-to-face class where students have space to walk around and talk with each other.

Online Synchronous

--

Online Asynchronous

--

Topic Areas

Anatomy & physiology

Kinesiology

Pathophysiology

Clinical reasoning

Ethics

Learning Stage Adaptation Examples

Review

This is an excellent review for important concepts. It can be done a few times in a term to help highlight important information the students will need to remember.

Application

Students construct an idea of their term through the series of questions.

Integration

This activity can be helpful at the beginning of an advanced course to help students recall foundational material that will be built upon in that class.

Diversity Considerations

This activity offers a nice opportunity for peer tutoring as students engage with each other and try to think of questions. In cases where students really struggle, the instructor and other students can suggest questions to ask. At the conclusion of the activity, each student can share what information or question was essential to identify the information on their nametag.

HANDS OFF!

Poker

This vocabulary building activity is also based on a party game. Working in two (or more) small groups, students use index cards to create a deck of terms for the other group(s). The deck of terms should equal about 5-8 cards for each student in the class. The terms should all be from the same unit or course module—to help the students with review.

The completed deck—with all cards facing down—is shuffled and passed to another group. Once each group has a new deck, one student deals the deck facedown to all students in that group so they all have the same number of cards.

The instructor says "Go" and each student holds a card up to their forehead. They can see all cards except their own. Students take turns asking yes or no questions from the members of their group to identify their term. When they guess the correct term, they put down their card. Once all students have guessed correctly, each student draws a new card and the game repeats.

Materials and Implementation

Blank index cards, pens/pencils.

Face-to-Face

This activity is designed for a face-to-face class where students have space to walk around and talk with each other.

Online Synchronous

--

Online Asynchronous

--

Topic Areas

Anatomy & physiology

Kinesiology

Pathophysiology

Learning Stage Adaptation Examples
Review
This is an excellent vocabulary-building exercise. Building the deck provides an opportunity to review.
Application
Students construct an idea of their term by looking at other terms in their small group.
Integration
--

Diversity Considerations

This activity offers a nice opportunity for peer tutoring as students engage with each other and try to guess their term. In cases where students really struggle the other students can suggest questions to ask. At the conclusion of the activity, each student can share which terms are easy to remember, and why.

Team-Based Learning

Jigsaw 1

This activity involves small groups using peer teaching, cooperation, and collaboration to explore a complex problem. The activity requires a minimum of three groups and involves three stages.

Stage 1: Each small group of students is designated as "experts" and tasked with investigating a different aspect of the larger problem. Within each group, students work together to acquire information. All participants should prepare notes.

Stage 2: New groups are configured as working groups with students from each Stage 1 group distributed among the new groups. Each student in the reconfigured group has different expertise. As a working group, students share what they learned in Stage 1 to collectively prepare a solution to the larger problem.

Stage 3: Each Stage 2 group presents their solution to the class. Once all solutions are presented, the class can compare and contrast the solutions.

Materials and Implementation

The number of categories of required "expertise" should equal the number of students in each group to ensure all students participate. To use time efficiently, the Stage 1 work could be required as pre-work before the class meeting.

Face-to-Face

This activity works nicely in class with space to configure students in small groups.

Online Synchronous

This could work using breakout rooms.

Online Asynchronous

--

Topic Areas
Pathophysiology
Clinical reasoning

Learning Stage Adaptation Examples

Review

--

Application

This is an excellent opportunity for students to organize foundational information into resources to present a case scenario. Examples:
- Asthma. Stage 1 groups identify risk factors, pathophysiology, functional limitations, and treatments. Stage 2 groups would use that information to construct a case scenario.
- Preeclampsia. Stage 1 groups identify risk factors, pathophysiology, potential complications, and treatments. Stage 2 groups would use that information to construct a case scenario.

Integration

This activity could be an initial stage to help students utilize information to form a treatment plan. Examples:
- Degenerative disc disease. Stage 1 groups could examine risk factors, pathophysiology, symptoms, and assessments. Stage 2 groups would use that information to design a treatment plan.
- Plantar fasciitis. Stage 1 groups could identify risk factors, symptoms, assessments, and self-care approaches. Stage 2 groups would use that information to create a treatment plan.

Diversity Considerations

Students who have difficulty speaking up in class may need encouragement to share within their group. Each student's part is essential. It provides an opportunity to teach cooperation, listening skills, and presentation skills. Depending upon agreement within groups, students may need to negotiate on the solution they will present to the class.

Jigsaw 2

This variation on the jigsaw activity follows a slightly different process through three stages.

Stage 1: Students from home groups and are presented with a large problem. Within each group, they summarize expertise that they need to propose a solution. Then, each student is assigned a role to go seek expertise.

Stage 2: New groups are formed that gather students seeking specific expertise. Each expert group works together to acquire information to inform their particular area of the larger question. All participants should prepare notes.

Stage 3: Students return to their home group and share their expertise. The group outlines a solution to the problem. Each group presents their solution to the class. Once all solutions are presented, the class can compare and contrast the solutions.

Materials and Implementation

To use time efficiently, the Stage 1 work could be required as pre-work before the class meeting.

Face-to-Face

This activity works nicely in class with space to configure students in small groups.

Online Synchronous

This could work using breakout rooms.

Online Asynchronous

This could be modified to have students work in a collaborative document and prepare a video presentation for the final stage.

Topic Areas

Pathophysiology

Clinical reasoning

Learning Stage Adaptation Examples

Review

--

Application

This is an excellent opportunity for students to organize foundational information into resources to present a case scenario. Examples:

— Migraine: Stage 1 groups review the larger problem and summarize what they know about risk factors, pathophysiology, symptoms and treatments. Stage 2 groups are formed to examine each of these four areas. In Stage 3, students return to their original group, share information, and use the information to construct a case scenario.

Integration

This activity could be an initial stage to help students utilize information to form a treatment plan. Examples:

— Fibromyalgia: Stage 1 groups would review the larger problem and summarize what they know about risk factors, symptoms, assessments, and self-care approaches. Stage 2 groups would examine each of these four areas. In Stage 3 students would return to their original group, share information, and use it to create a treatment plan.

Diversity Considerations

The number of categories of required "expertise" should equal the number of students in each group to ensure all students participate.

Students who have difficulty speaking up in class may need encouragement to share within their group. Each student's part is essential. It provides an opportunity to teach cooperation, listening skills, and presentation skills. Depending upon agreement within groups, students may need to negotiate on the solution they will present to the class.

Debate Club 1

Debating can foster critical thinking, promote cooperation and collaboration, encourage students to listen, and build presentation skills. A debate is a formal argument involving expression of different viewpoints. In order for a debate to be successful, a controversial topic should be selected that has two (or more) sides to an argument. Students can be assigned a perspective to debate. That is especially important when using topics for which most of the class would be in agreement.

For a Fishbowl Debate, two small teams of students debate in front of the class. Each group is assigned a position in relation to the argument and presents their opening statement. Then the remainder of the class can ask questions so each team can clarify or support their position. At the conclusion of the questions and answers, the class votes on the winner of the debate: the team that presented the most persuasive argument.

Materials and Implementation

Students should be given the topic ahead of time to allow preparation. Having course materials and other references on-hand can help students frame their argument and provide evidence to defend their position.

Face-to-Face

This is an engaging activity for a face-to-face class.

Online Synchronous

This can be done online having small groups present to the class.

Online Asynchronous

--

Topic Areas

Clinical reasoning

Ethics

Learning Stage Adaptation Examples
Review

--

Application

This activity can be helpful when it requires students to analyze and interpret information to frame their argument and support their answer. Example:
— Treatment prices and access to care for underserved communities

Integration

This activity can be designed to encourage students to draw upon research evidence to support their argument. Example:
— Successful clinical trials should be required for any intervention offered or performed by a healthcare professional.

Diversity Considerations

Assigning roles in a debate requires students to be objective rather than working from their own beliefs and assumptions. This can be challenging for novice learners. Encouraging students to access information to support their argument can help them more effectively use resource material.

Debate Club 2

Mini debates can engage the whole class in exploration of an issue that has two different sides. The whole class is divided into groups of three. Two group members (debaters) are assigned different sides of the argument; the third group member is the judge. Within their group each student summarizes their position. Then the judge asks questions to allow them to clarify or further support their position. At the conclusion of the small group, each judge secretly writes down the winner of the debate.

The class comes together and the judge from each group reports back to the class to summarize the arguments presented by the debaters. After each judge is finished reporting, all judges reveal who won the debate in their group.

Materials and Implementation

Students should be given the topic ahead of time to allow for preparation. Having course materials and other references on hand can help students frame their argument and provide evidence to defend their position.

Face-to-Face

This is an engaging activity for a face-to-face class.

Online Synchronous

This can be done online using breakout rooms for small groups.

Online Asynchronous

--

Topic Areas
Clinical reasoning
Ethics

Learning Stage Adaptation Examples

Review

--

Application

This activity can be helpful when it requires students to analyze and interpret information to frame their argument and support their answer. Example:
— Should selling products directly to patients be illegal?

Integration

This activity can be designed to encourage students to draw upon research evidence to support their argument. Example:
— Use of informal language interpreters (i.e. family members or friends that are not trained in interpretation for healthcare) in treatment settings

Diversity Considerations

Some students may be uncomfortable in a controversial conversation. Take care to ensure that the discussion stays focused on the argument and supporting evidence is provided to support each student's position.

Students who are competitive by nature may be more focused on winning than creating a well-thought-out answer. The instructor can de-emphasize the competitive aspect of the activity by highlighting the key components from each report.

Group work can easily get sidetracked. To keep small groups focused, the instructor can listen in on each group in turn and provide guidance if needed.

Debate Club 3

A Four Corners debate is similar to a caucus. It is a debate on a statement that could be interpreted four different ways: Students form groups based upon their response to a statement. Then each group aims to draw students from other groups to joint them. Each interpretation must be supported by a valid argument. Examples:

— Clients are truthful about their health.
— Stress increases perception of pain.
— Discomfort should be tolerated.

Possible responses: always, sometimes, rarely, never are each assigned a corner of the classroom. The instructor reads the statement. Students are given a few moments to decide, then they move to the corner that aligns with their answer. Students in each corner form a team and are given time to work as a group to prepare an argument to defend their answer.

Each group then presents their argument to the whole class. After all arguments are presented, all students have the option to move to another corner to align with a different answer. The corner with the most students wins the debate.

Materials and Implementation

Students can be given possible topics ahead of time to prepare.

Face-to-Face

This is an engaging activity for a face-to-face class.

Online Synchronous

--

Online Asynchronous

This could be adapted to have students respond to a discussion forum to defend their opinion.

Topic Areas
Clinical reasoning
Ethics

Learning Stage Adaptation Examples
Review

--

Application

This activity can be helpful when it requires students to analyze and interpret information to frame their argument and support their answer.

Integration

This activity can be designed to encourage students to draw upon research evidence to support their argument.

Diversity Considerations

Strong leaders may be persuasive in gathering other students to their position. The instructor could go around to each group (prior to the presentations) and encourage all group members to align with the argument they feel most capable of defending.

Students may feel swayed to join their friends rather than taking a position in relation to the activity. One way to encourage students to think independently is to ask every student to be prepared to summarize in a single sentence why they chose their location. Calling on a few students may help others feel empowered to move to the group that is more aligned with their answer.

HANDS OFF!

Team Quiz

This activity uses a team-based approach for review and practice tests. It works best with test questions that are complex or tricky. The instructor should prepare a series of multiple-choice quiz questions and answers. The class is separated into small groups. Each group needs four sheets of paper: each with a letter corresponding to a multiple-choice answer (A, B, C, D) written large enough for the whole class to see.

The instructor poses a question with answer choices. The class is given 1-2 minutes to agree upon the best answer. The instructor calls "Time" and a representative from each group holds up the letter corresponding to that group's answer. Before revealing which answer was correct, each group is asked to defend their answer.

Materials and Implementation

A prepared series of questions and answers.

Face-to-Face

This is an engaging activity for a face-to-face class that could be used regularly to help students review for an exam.

Online Synchronous

--

Online Asynchronous

This could be modified to give all questions to small groups, allow students time to collaborate and then submit their answers to the instructor along with a short video defense. Videos can be shared with the entire class and the correct answer revealed.

Topic Areas

Pathophysiology

Clinical reasoning

Ethics

Learning Stage Adaptation Examples

Review

This is an excellent activity to include on an ongoing basis at the end of course units or modules. It provides a review and encourages peer teaching. A session with 3 to 5 questions can be completed in a relatively short amount of time.

Application

This activity can use questions that require students to draw upon foundational concepts to solve more complex problems.

Integration

This activity can promote critical thinking if case-based scenarios are used for the question stem and treatment options are potential answers.

Diversity Considerations

Eager students may overshadow slower learners or quieter students in this type of activity. All students will need time to learn how to effectively participate. Encouraging students to use inclusive approaches will give all opportunities for participation. Strategies like taking turns, speaking first, and polling within the group for the answer can give all students a chance to contribute.

Case-Based Learning

Clinic Role-Play

Role-play is spontaneous, contextualized simulation where students take on a persona for a learning activity. The objective can be improving active listening skills, gathering information through interviewing, and/or demonstrating professionalism. Students work in pairs or small groups with one student assigned to the role of "Client" and the other(s) "Practitioner." For the role of Client, students are given background information or a scenario. They may also complete a health history form. The Practitioner interviews the Client to gather information. This requires the Client to provide accurate responses based upon the scenario.

The activity can assign each Client a different problem from the course unit or module. Alternatively, all Clients could have the same health problem that affects different personas. After the role-play, the Practitioners can share what they learned from their Clients.

Materials and Implementation

Face-to-Face

This works well in a face-to-face class with adequate space that can be arranged to allow students to conduct interviews.

Online Synchronous

This could be modified to have pairs of students demonstrating role-play for the class.

Online Asynchronous

This could be modified to be an assignment. Clients could submit completed health history forms; a list of written interview questions could be exchanged, and Practitioners could submit written case reports.

Topic Areas

Pathophysiology

Clinical reasoning

Learning Stage Adaptation Examples

Review

This activity can be used to help students recognize essential information to present (in the role of Client) or extract (in the role of Practitioner) in a case scenario.

Application

The "practitioner" could be required to identify assessments that they would perform to gather additional information.

Integration

The "practitioner" could be required to create a treatment plan including assessments and anticipated outcomes of treatment

Diversity Considerations

This type of activity requires students to think spontaneously while providing accurate information. That may be challenging for slower learners. Encouraging all students to be mindful of their partner can promote a quality learning experience.

Students may have difficulty with the concept of a persona. Focusing on the active-listening skills and the essential information can help students recognize the learning potential in this type of activity.

Threaded Case Scenario

A threaded case scenario requires students to follow the same case over a period of time. The basic case scenario is introduced at the beginning of the course, unit, or module. Then it is revisited at regular intervals for the duration of the course, unit, or module. As students acquire new knowledge, they learn to apply it to the scenario. The entire class can work with a single case or each student can be assigned a different case.

A range of activities can be used for the reviews including having the students write interview questions, identify relevant information, list assessments, or explore treatment options. Students could also be assigned a research project on risk factors or effectiveness of different treatments.

Materials and Implementation

Face-to-Face

This activity can be a combination of self-directed work and in class discussion with students working in small groups to present cases to each other.

Online Synchronous

This can be modified online to have students taking turns presenting their case to the class during the course unit or module.

Online Asynchronous

This activity could use a combination of independent assignments and prompts in a discussion forum.

Topic Areas

Anatomy & physiology

Kinesiology

Pathophysiology

Clinical reasoning

Ethics

Learning Stage Adaptation Examples

Review

This activity can be used to help students recognize essential information to extract from a case scenario.
- Case introduction: underline key words or identify essential information.
- Case revisited: identify information from the course that supplements or changes their initial assessment.
- Case conclusion: review again and finalize what they believe is relevant information about the case.

Application

This can be used to help students take a structured approach to assessment of a case.
- Case introduction: identify essential information.
- Case revisited: identify information from the course that provides a deeper level of insight into the case.
- Case conclusion: summarize the case.

Integration

This can be used as a critical thinking exercise where students apply what they learned to solve a problem related to the case.
- Case introduction: identify essential information.
- Case revisited: outline questions aimed at revealing more information to inform their knowledge about the case.
- Case conclusion: review and make a recommendation for the case.

Diversity Considerations

This activity can help students recognize their own progress as they learn new concepts and apply them to a familiar scenario. This is helpful for students who struggle with relevance of course material. Having students work in small groups to present to each other and collectively problem solve can benefit presentation and collaboration skills.

Case Across the Curriculum

A case scenario can be integrated across multiple courses to help students integrate and apply concepts from different areas of the curriculum. The basic case scenario is introduced in a foundational class. Then it is revisited in subsequent classes. As students acquire new knowledge, they apply it to the scenario. To facilitate discussion, a few case scenarios can be assigned to different sectors of the class. As students work with the cases in different classes, assignments and activities can be individualized or involve small groups.

A range of activities can be used to review the case through didactic and clinical courses. Students can extract essential information, write interview questions, engage in role-play (in the role of the case or a practitioner), list assessments, or explore treatment options. As a capstone project, students could complete a research paper and presentation relative to something about the case. Instructors should be briefed on the cases and have input on activities.

Materials and Implementation

Face-to-Face

This activity can involve discussions at regular intervals.

Online Synchronous

Forums can be used to hold small group discussions.

Online Asynchronous

Discussion forums can be used to have students review cases.

Topic Areas

Anatomy & physiology

Pathophysiology

Clinical reasoning

Ethics

CASE-BASED LEARNING

Learning Stage Adaptation Examples

Review

Introduce the case in anatomy & physiology to provide context for body systems review. Examples:
- 42-year-old male with degenerative disc disease
- 53-year-old female with osteopenia
- 11-year-old male with muscular dystrophy
- 15-year-old female with cystic fibrosis

Application

Revisit the case in kinesiology or pathophysiology to summarize:
- Risk factors
- Structural and functional changes and abnormalities
- Signs, symptoms
- Treatment options

Integration

Revisit the case in practicum and/or ethics to identify:
- Potential ethical issues related to care and treatment
- Assessments for direct and indirect effects of treatment
- Treatment plan design

Diversity Considerations

This type of activity can help students contextualize complicated healthcare issues. Including case scenarios that have risk factors related to genetics, sex, and race can provide opportunity to discuss cultural competence in client care.

Requiring students to follow the same case through different areas of the curriculum can provide examples for students who struggle to apply and integrate information.

Creative Case Scenarios

Case-based learning offers rich opportunities in learning through review of material, application of concepts, and integration of ideas. When cases are written or chosen specifically for learning purposes, they sometimes present an ideal or stereotypical scenario. While this may be helpful for novice learners, it does not necessarily serve advanced students. Case-based learning that approximates real world scenarios provides a low-stakes way for students to hone critical thinking skills and integrate concepts from courses throughout the curriculum.

Often, case-based learning requires students to gather information to propose a solution. In a grand rounds format the class works as a single group to review a case. When some students are more vocal than others, the grand rounds format may not stimulate adequate discussion in a way that involves all students in the activity. This is especially challenging when the case seeks a single answer or resolution that can be provided by one student. Having students create case scenarios from an existing resource broadens the opportunity for participation. Creative case scenario assignments can be structured to require either an inductive reasoning approach or deductive reasoning. Both can be helpful to practice observation skills and attention to detail.

Writing multiple cases places a burden on the instructor. This approach offers a solution that provides a learning opportunity for students. Organization using a scaffolding approach is essential for the success of creative case scenarios. This begins with identifying source material, writing and revising the case scenario, presenting the case, and using it for learning activities.

Case Selection

Each student should use a unique case to provide variety and also build a library of cases for the course. For a course (or an assignment) the instructor first chooses a category from which the case is selected. Then each student identifies the character, figure, or resource they will use for their case. These should be shared with the class to ensure that there is no duplication of the same case by multiple students.

Using publicly-available information and sources for cases is essential to maintain ethical boundaries. Students can work with information supplied by

CASE-BASED LEARNING

the source and supplement using course material. As students write their case they will need to make assumptions based upon the information they can access. This presents the opportunity for students to apply and integrate course material and engage in critical thinking.

Selecting different categories of sources for case material for different assignments or classes eliminates the possibility that a student would try to use the same case in multiple classes. It also minimizes the potential that a student could obtain an assignment completed by a student in a previous class.

Popular Culture

Writers take great care creating characters that have depth, personalities, individual motives, struggles, and context. Characters also have physical description. For performance, actors are cast based upon physical description of characters. Building case scenarios using characters from books (adult fiction, young adult fiction, and children's books), film, television, or plays provide the opportunity to leverage existing material and build upon it. Examples:

— The television detective Adrian Monk was played with signs characteristic of obsessive-compulsive disorder.
— Walter White (in the television series *Breaking Bad*) had a diagnosis of lung cancer.
— John Stone (from the HBO series *The Night of*) has eczema.
— Eeyore (the donkey in the *Winnie the Pooh* books) exhibits symptoms of clinical depression.
— Red, from Phil Bildner's *Rip and Red* book series has autism spectrum disorder.
— William Shakespeare's Lady Macbeth walked in her sleep.

Biography or History

Biographies and autobiographies provide realistic presentations that can be used for case study. Books often reveal complex details related to risk factors, diagnosis, or treatment including the subject's physical, psychoemotional, environmental, social, or genetic characteristics.

— Lena Dunham's autobiography, *Not That Kind of Girl* describes her struggles with disordered eating.

HANDS OFF!

- In his autobiography, *Lucky Man*, Michael J. Fox, reflects on his struggles with Parkinson's disease.
- Jill Bolte Taylor's *My Stroke of Insight* provides a highly detailed account of the experience of a stroke and the recovery process.
- The film *A Beautiful Mind* is a biography of John Forbes Nash, Jr. who lived with schizophrenia.
- Julius Caesar is reported to have had epilepsy.
- Ludwig van Beethoven slowly lost his hearing, possibly to Paget Disease.
- Abraham Lincoln had physical characteristics associated with Marfan Syndrome.

Bloggers

Coping with a disease or illness can make a person physically, psychologically, and emotionally vulnerable. Some patients elect to share their experiences publicly. Blogs can provide personal, informal insights into an individual's experience with a disease or disorder. Bloggers have different motivations to share their stories. They may find writing to be cathartic, reflective, or a way to express themselves. A blogger may want others to learn from their experience.

It is important to note that blogs should be used only if they are publicly available, written on an open website that does not require membership, login, or password for the reader. Although a blogger using this type of format does not have an expectation of privacy, confidentiality should be maintained when the blog is used to construct a case scenario.

An instructor using a blog as a resource should take into account that information shared in a blog is not verified or fact checked. Blogs are entirely subjective and can provide insight into a patient's experience.

To find blogs, students can do general internet searches for specific diseases or disorders. In order for a blog to be useful in building a case, it should be lengthy (at least 1000 words if a single entry, or have multiple entries posted over a series of time) and have adequate information to get to know the subject. Blogs that primarily post pictures or videos are not a good case upon which to build a scenario if they do not involve the subject providing substantial or ongoing insight into their health and well-being.

CASE-BASED LEARNING

The source should be provided for purposes of verification for the assignment, but the name of the blogger and other identifying information should be removed in reporting. No attempts should be made to contact the author of the blog.

Case Writing

Students prepare their case scenario. It can be structured as a narrative, presented as a completed clinic form, or other format used elsewhere in the curriculum. For interdisciplinary courses students can present their case using the format from their own discipline which creates an opportunity for interprofessional education. The instructor can grade this as an assignment and the cases can then be used for course activities.

Case-Based Learning

Students can work individually, in pairs, or in small groups. They can present and refine their own case scenarios and use the case for a learning activity. Case scenarios can be passed around to different students or groups in the class to provide opportunities to explore different cases. Potential activities include clinic role-play, interpretation, and analysis of a case, identifying relevant assessments, writing interview questions, and/or developing treatment plans. Graded activities can include presentation of the case, developing interview questions, proposing assessments, or developing treatment plans.

Materials and Implementation

Face-to-Face

Cases can be prepared as low-stakes assignments and then used for individual student presentations or small group activities. Case-based activities can be scheduled at regular intervals to help students become familiar with case review, discussion, and presentation.

Online Synchronous

This can be adapted for an online class to promote small group discussion. Students can post their cases to a discussion forum for all to review. During live class breakout rooms can be used for small group presentation and discussion. That could be followed by a spokesperson from the small group reporting back to the class with a summary presentation.

Online Asynchronous

Discussion forums can be used to have students present cases to each other and review cases.

Students could prepare video presentations of their cases to the class for review and discussion.

Collaborative documents could be used for small groups of students to draft interview questions or prepare treatment plans.

Topic Areas

Anatomy & physiology

Kinesiology

Pathophysiology

Clinical reasoning

Ethics

Almost any area of the massage and bodywork education curriculum lends itself to creating and working with case scenarios. It is relatively common that questions about health, risk factors, and disease or illness arise during a student's education. Using existing information as cases and encouraging students to explore information can be an effective way to help them apply course concepts. This is especially helpful for material from foundational courses if students have difficulty recognizing relevance of information that is difficult to learn.

Learning Stage Adaptation Examples

Review

Create cases in pathophysiology, practicum, or ethics to provide context for clinical presentation.

Application

Create cases in kinesiology or pathophysiology to review
- Known or suspected risk factors
- Anticipated structural and functional changes and abnormalities
- Clinical presentation, signs, symptoms
- Treatment options

Integration

Revisit the case in practicum and/or ethics to identify:
- — Potential ethical issues related to care and treatment
- — Assessments for direct and indirect effects of treatment
- — Treatment plan design

Diversity Considerations

Students have the opportunity to seek subjects for their cases that are of interest to them or have a personal connection. Encouraging students to consider sources relevant to their own community, culture, or personal background can provide an opportunity to inject cultural competence into learning activities that use the cases.

For students who have difficulty speaking up in class the opportunity to work with partners or small groups gives a lower-stakes environment to present and get feedback.

When students have difficulty thinking on their feet, the case discussion may initially be challenging. Allowing the opportunity to revisit the case at different intervals can help students refine ideas and layer course concepts.

Appendix

Appendix A: Sample Lesson Plans

Got Your Back as an Icebreaker

At the beginning of a new term when students will need to draw upon foundation material from a previous course use *Got Your Back* as an icebreaker and a review.

The instructor can welcome students at the classroom entrance and place the name tags on their backs.

For the first 10-15 minutes of class the students can play the game by asking questions while they find their seats, get settled, and greet each other.

The formal class session can begin even if everyone has not yet finished the game. When there is a break in class, students can continue to work on trying to identify their term. If some student really struggle, the instructor can help with prompts.

Once every student has identified their term and moved their nametag to their chest, the class can review. For the reflection/debriefing, the instructor can share the full list of terms and remind students that they are responsible to know the terms used in the game and integrate information from previous courses.

APPENDIX

Review with Calisthenics 2

Calisthenics 2 can be used to review the joints, actions, and muscles of the lower extremity.

Prior to class, students should be asked to dress in exercise-friendly clothing and footwear.

To prepare for the class, arrange the classroom with adequate space for movement. When students arrive, store books, bags, and coats off to the side. Have the students stand in a circle or in rows (like an exercise class.)

Invite them to march in place. Then ask them to say the movements of the hip joint as they perform them. While they are still marching focus next on the knee joint, then the ankle joint.

Pause.

Then start again with Jumping Jacks. Ask them again to call the movement of the hip as they move, then the knee, then the ankle.

Pause.

Invite them to share what is similar to—or different from—marching in place.

Then start again with squats and ask them to call the hip as they move, then the knee, and ankle.

Stop.

Invite them to compare and contrast how major joints of the lower extremity produce movement.

For the reflection/debriefing, ask the students to assume their typical position in class and make a list of the muscles that produce different movements of the hip, knee, and ankle.

HANDS OFF!

Study Skills using A *Little Help Here*

To start a review at the end of a course unit or module use *A Little Help Here*.

The instructor can begin class with a brief summary while blank index cards are handed out to the class.

Then students have 2-3 minutes to write one topic on their card that needs further explanation.

Students hand cards back to the instructor, the cards are shuffled and randomly distributed back to students.

The class spends 15 minutes working in small groups to identify resource material (e.g. a specific lecture, book chapter, assigned reading, or internet resource) they would use to answer the question and writes the name of the resource on the back of the card. Then each group reports the questions and suggestions back to the class.

The cards can be handed back to the instructor.

For the reflection/debriefing, the instructor can summarize the most common areas that students identify needing further explanation.

Prior to the end of class, the instructor can place the cards original topic facing up—on a table near the classroom exit. Students can pick up their card as they leave.

APPENDIX

<u>Review with Mind Your MCQs</u>

Running a review session prior to a high-stakes exam can be helpful. Instead of summarizing everything for the class, incorporate *Mind Your MCQs*.

Begin by breaking the class into small groups. Remind them of the lectures, chapters, and other material that will be covered on the exam.

Then give them 15-20 minutes to write 5 multiple choice test questions.

Bring the class back together and have each group take turns testing the whole class with one of their questions.

For the reflection/debriefing ask the students to share why they identified specific information as important enough to warrant a test question.

At the end of class, ask a spokesperson for each group to type their questions into a shared document or discussion forum in the Learning Management System. This will create a practice test for the class.

Appendix B: Sample Assessments

Graded Rubric

A rubric can provide feedback for students based upon expectations for participation in the activity. For collaborative activities like *Rowing Team* or *Strips in Sequence*, create a scale using words for the range of assessment (e.g. Needs Improvement, Adequate, Above Average, Excellent.) Include a numerical rating for each to provide students with a score.

For active learning, possible items for assessment on a rubric include:
- Stayed focused on the activity
- Shared responsibility with group
- Made individual contribution to group success
- Managed time well
- Listened to group members
- Respected other opinions

Instructors should review and return completed rubrics to students as soon as possible after the activity so the students can reflect on what they did well along with areas for improvement.

APPENDIX

Student Self-Assessment

A rubric can be created that gives students the opportunity to self-assess their behavior and participation in the activity. This can be very helpful for games like *In a Flash* and *Poker*. Using a scale with categories can facilitate self-assessment in group activities (e.g. Novice, Contributor, Master, Expert.)

Assigning a number to each category can provide the students with an overall score to monitor their progress. Possible items for behavioral assessment include:

— Met learning objectives
— Took activity seriously
— Time management
— Ability to make opinions known
— Negotiation skills
— Resourcefulness
— Inclusiveness

The instructor can collect these assessments during the course, and at the end of the term, each student can be provided with all of their assessments to review. They can then be asked to summarize areas where they made progress along with areas that still need improvement.

For group activities students can be asked to summarize their major role or contribution. They can also be asked to identify their percent of effort and how that related to the overall effort of the group. Students in a group of 4 would be expected to contribute approximately 25% effort or in a group of 5 contribute near 20% effort.

HANDS OFF!

Grading Materials

Some strategies for active learning involve creation of materials as part of the activity. *Physical Assessment Protocol, Three Questions, In a Flash,* and *Creative Case Scenarios* are examples of activities that produce something. Students can receive credit for attendance when they participate in the class activity. But the produced materials can also be graded as an assignment. This can provide a relatively low-stakes way to assess performance. Planning is essential so that the contribution to the overall course grade has been calculated ahead of time. The active learning session and the assignment should be listed in the syllabus and course outline.

APPENDIX

Appendix C: Ideas for Reflection or Evaluation

Open-ended questions or scoring sheets can be used for reflections and evaluations of active learning sessions. These can be delivered informally by asking the class for general feedback. Alternatively, brief surveys can be given to students immediately following each session.

Topics for Reflection

- The most important thing learned in the activity
- How the activity was challenging
- What our group did that worked well
- One way this activity helped me grow
- What I would do differently next time to make this a better experience for my group
- My biggest contribution to the group's success
- How I can record what I learned in this activity in my course notes

Topics for Evaluation

- Clarity of instructions
- Session organization
- Suggestions for preparation was adequate to help me fully participate
- My time was used effectively
- There was adequate time to complete the activity
- The extent to which the activity was easy or challenging
- Ability to get help or feedback
- Availability of resources needed to complete the activity

Index

Active learning, 2, 3, 4, 5, 6, 7, 8, 9, 10, 11, 181, 183, 184
Advanced course, 118, 144
Affective, 3, 4
Anatomy, 5, 9, 10, 11, 15, 17, 36, 65, 76, 82, 90, 168
Anatomy & physiology, 9, 11, 82, 90, 168
Assessment, 5, 7, 11, 37, 40, 59, 60, 63, 64, 67, 80, 83, 91, 92, 93, 94, 100, 113, 114, 118, 120, 166, 181, 182, 183
Attendance, 7, 183
Balance, 32, 34, 57, 72, 106
Base of support, 16, 18, 20, 22, 26, 32, 34, 44, 46, 48, 58, 60
Bloom, 3, 4
Breakout rooms, 9, 51, 53, 55, 57, 73, 93, 97, 105, 109, 115, 117, 121, 131, 137, 149, 151, 155, 172
Cards, 25, 27, 36, 39, 81, 99, 117, 134, 136, 139, 140, 141, 145, 179
Case, 5, 6, 8, 10, 71, 72, 73, 74, 83, 84, 94, 98, 128, 150, 152, 160, 163, 164, 165, 166, 167, 168, 169, 170, 171, 172, 174, 183
Cognitive, 3, 4, 9

Collaborate, 2, 82, 97, 107, 120, 128, 132, 159
Collaborative document, 71, 73, 77, 79, 87, 89, 91, 93, 97, 101, 117, 131, 151
Communication, 5, 7, 11, 124
Compare and contrast, 23, 25, 29, 45, 46, 47, 49, 51, 55, 59, 75, 80, 87, 89, 107, 120, 122, 124, 128, 149, 151, 178
Computer, 87, 89, 91, 93, 103
Definitions, 3, 10, 77, 78, 98, 128, 142
Didactic, 2, 3, 4, 78, 80, 98, 102, 116, 167
Discussion forum, 15, 43, 45, 47, 49, 51, 53, 55, 57, 71, 73, 93, 103, 107, 115, 121, 165, 172, 180
Disorder, 11, 28, 63, 170, 171
Exercise mat, 21, 23, 25, 35
Flashcard, 142
Footwear, 15, 17, 19, 21, 23, 25, 27, 29, 31, 33, 35, 37, 45, 178
Formative, 2, 5, 11
Foundational, 3, 68, 98, 102, 116, 118, 142, 144, 150, 152, 160, 167
Glossary, 77, 78, 98, 128, 134, 136, 140

Informal, 2, 7, 67, 83, 105, 113, 114, 118, 156, 171
Leadership, 5, 101
Low-tech, 137, 139, 142
Memory, 99, 110
Muscles, 16, 18, 19, 22, 26, 28, 29, 30, 34, 36, 38, 46, 54, 56, 60, 62, 65, 66, 76, 104, 110, 116, 128, 131, 132, 178
Novice, 2, 15, 26, 98, 154, 169, 182
Pair of students, 31, 33, 35, 123, 133, 135, 141
Present, 3, 7, 43, 51, 53, 55, 57, 58, 83, 87, 89, 93, 150, 152, 153, 164, 165, 166, 169, 172, 173, 174
Presentation, 6, 57, 83, 84, 103, 116, 132, 150, 151, 152, 153, 166, 167, 172, 173, 174
Psychomotor, 3, 4, 81
Quality of life, 93, 94, 106
Reflect, 2, 6, 28, 30, 32, 34, 40, 46, 68, 92, 115, 181
Reflection, 4, 7, 34, 44, 46, 67, 103, 177, 178, 179, 180
Research, 4, 46, 90, 93, 105, 106, 154, 156, 158, 165, 167
Review, 2, 3, 6, 7, 9, 10, 11, 16, 17, 18, 19, 21, 26, 28, 33, 34, 35, 36, 43, 44, 46, 48, 49, 50, 52, 53, 54, 56, 58, 59, 60, 63, 65, 68, 74, 75, 77, 78, 80, 81, 82, 83, 84, 88, 91, 94, 97, 99, 100, 101, 102, 104, 105, 106, 107, 108, 113, 114, 116, 118, 121, 128, 129, 130, 137, 139, 140, 141, 142, 144, 145, 146, 152, 159, 160, 166, 167, 168, 169, 172, 173, 177, 178, 179, 180, 181, 182
Role-play, 3, 4, 5, 9, 123, 163, 167, 172
Small groups, 5, 8, 11, 37, 43, 47, 49, 51, 53, 55, 57, 67, 73, 80, 81, 87, 89, 91, 92, 93, 97, 99, 100, 105, 106, 107, 109, 110, 115, 116, 121, 137, 139, 140, 145, 149, 153, 155, 156, 159, 163, 165, 166, 167, 172, 173, 174, 179, 180
Study guide, 9, 80, 97, 98
Tablet, 79, 87, 89, 91, 93, 97, 101, 105, 109
Tests, 2, 3, 44, 48, 99, 104, 109, 110, 120, 141, 159
Tutoring, 11, 103, 142, 144, 146
Webcams, 17, 19, 21, 23, 25, 27, 113, 129
Whiteboard, 8, 77, 79, 115, 137
Writing, 67, 71, 73, 169, 172

About the Author

Virginia S. Cowen, PhD is a researcher, writer, and educator with over 20 years' experience in health, fitness and wellness. She has been a member of the faculty at Rutgers University, the University of Medicine and Dentistry of New Jersey, and Queensborough Community College. Dr. Cowen earned her PhD in curriculum and instruction with a concentration in exercise and wellness from Arizona State University. She is a Google Certified Educator Level 1 and Level 2. She has served on the board of directors for the Alliance for Massage Therapy Education, the leadership development committee for the National Certification Board for Therapeutic Massage and Bodywork, and as a reviewer for the Massage Therapy Foundation. She is a licensed massage therapist and holds certifications as a yoga teacher, Pilates teacher, strength and conditioning specialist, and personal trainer. Dr. Cowen is passionate about education innovation.

Other Books by Virginia S. Cowen, PhD

Beyond Lectures: Engaging Distance Learning for Massage and Bodywork Education —Pennate Press

101 Cases for Study in Massage and Bodywork Education —Pennate Press

101 Cases for Study in Exercise Science and Personal Training —Pennate Press

101 Cases for Study in Pilates Teacher Training —Pennate Press

101 Cases for Study in Yoga Teacher Training —Pennate Press

Hands Off! 70 Active Learning Strategies for Pilates Teacher Training —Pennate Press

Hands Off! 70 Active Learning Strategies for Exercise Science and Personal Training —Pennate Press

Hands Off! 70 Active Learning Strategies for Yoga Teacher Training —Pennate Press

Pathophysiology for Massage Therapists: A Functional Approach —F.A. Davis

Therapeutic Massage and Bodywork for Autism Spectrum Disorders: A Guide for Parents and Caregivers—Singing Dragon Books

www.ingramcontent.com/pod-product-compliance
Lightning Source LLC
Chambersburg PA
CBHW060953230426
43665CB00015B/2186